M000009685

On Our Way to English®

Activity Book

Houghton Mifflin Harcourt

Copyright © by Houghton Mifflin Harcourt Publishing Company

All rights reserved. No part of this work may be reproduced or transmitted in any form or by any means, electronic or mechanical, including photocopying or recording, or by any information storage and retrieval system, without the prior written permission of the copyright owner unless such copying is expressly permitted by federal copyright law. Requests for permission to make copies of any part of the work should be addressed to Houghton Mifflin Harcourt Publishing Company, Attn: Contracts, Copyrights, and Licensing, 9400 Southpark Center Loop, Orlando, Florida 32819-8647.

Printed in the U.S.A.

ISBN 978-0-544-23540-3

2 3 4 5 6 7 8 9 10 1409 22 21 20 19 18 17 16 15 14
4500472067   A B C D E F G

If you have received these materials as examination copies free of charge, Houghton Mifflin Harcourt Publishing Company retains title to the materials and they may not be resold. Resale of examination copies is strictly prohibited.

Possession of this publication in print format does not entitle users to convert this publication, or any portion of it, into electronic format.

Contents

Teamwork 4

Word Recognition 8

Unit 1

Listening 9

Vocabulary 10

Speaking 12

Writing 13

Comprehension 17

Vocabulary 18

Grammar and Language 20

Comprehension 22

Fluency 23

Comprehension 24

Phonics and Spelling 26

Unit 2

Vocabulary 28

Writing 30

Comprehension 34

Vocabulary 35

Grammar and Language 37

Comprehension 39

Fluency 40

Comprehension 41

Phonics and Spelling 43

Unit 3

Vocabulary 45

Reading 47

Writing 48

Comprehension 52

Vocabulary 53

Grammar and Language 55

Comprehension 57

Fluency 58

Comprehension 59

Phonics and Spelling 61

© HMH Supplemental Publishers Inc.

Contents

Unit 4

Listening 63

Vocabulary 64

Speaking 66

Reading 67

Writing 68

Comprehension 72

Vocabulary 73

Grammar and Language 75

Comprehension 77

Fluency 78

Comprehension 79

Phonics and Spelling 81

Unit 5

Vocabulary 83

Reading 85

Writing 86

Comprehension 90

Vocabulary 91

Grammar and Language 93

Comprehension 95

Fluency 96

Comprehension 97

Phonics and Spelling 99

Unit 6

Vocabulary 101

Reading 103

Writing 104

Comprehension 108

Vocabulary 109

Grammar and Language 111

Comprehension 113

Fluency 114

Comprehension 115

Phonics and Spelling 117

© HMH Supplemental Publishers Inc.

Contents

Unit 7

Listening 119

Vocabulary 120

Speaking 122

Reading 123

Writing 124

Comprehension 128

Vocabulary 129

Grammar and Language 131

Comprehension 133

Fluency 134

Comprehension 135

Phonics and Spelling 137

Unit 8

Vocabulary 139

Reading 141

Writing 142

Comprehension 146

Vocabulary 147

Grammar and Language 149

Comprehension 151

Fluency 152

Comprehension 153

Phonics and Spelling 155

Grammar and Language
Handbook 157

Phonics and Spelling
Handbook 187

Check Your Progress 217

Index for Handbooks 222

Standardized Test-Taking
Tips 224

Practice Test 1 225

Practice Test 2 242

© HMH Supplemental Publishers Inc.

NAME _____

WHAT TO DO

If you can't think of a word . . .

point.

make a gesture.

draw a picture.

say it another way.

© HMH Supplemental Publishers Inc.

NAME _____

WAYS TO HELP

Be patient:
- with your words.
- with your expression.
- with your attitude.

Watch for cues:
- in actions.
- in gestures.
- in expressions.

© HMH Supplemental Publishers Inc.

Be encouraging by:
- asking questions.
- giving support.

NAME _____

WHAT TO DO

If you don't understand . . .

sit close to the teacher.

ask questions.

ask the speaker to slow down.

watch the speaker's mouth.
- This will help you understand.
- It will also help you with your pronunciation.

© HMH Supplemental Publishers Inc.

NAME _____

WAYS TO HELP

Act it out.

Lead the way.

Write it down.

Say it another way.

Be supportive.

© HMH Supplemental Publishers Inc.

Word Recognition

HIGH-FREQUENCY WORDS

 These are the most commonly used English words. Practice reading and spelling these words in order to become better readers and writers.

Unit 1	Unit 2	Unit 3	Unit 4
the	for	from	when
of	on	or	your
and	are	one	can
a	as	had	said
to	with	by	there
in	his	word	use
is	they	but	an
you	I	not	each
that	at	what	which
it	be	all	she
he	this	were	do
was	have	we	how

Unit 5	Unit 6	Unit 7	Unit 8
their	her	see	oil
if	would	number	sit
will	make	no	now
up	like	way	find
other	him	could	long
about	into	people	down
out	time	my	day
many	has	than	did
then	look	first	get
them	two	water	come
these	more	been	made
so	write	call	may
some	go	who	part

© HMH Supplemental Publishers Inc.

NAME _____

MONITORING LISTENING CHECKLIST

	Unit 1 Road to Freedom	Unit 2 By the People	Unit 3 Now Hear This!
1. What is the topic?			
2. I knew about the topic ____.	☐ already ☐ not at all	☐ already ☐ not at all	☐ already ☐ not at all
3. I knew most of the words ____.	☐ already ☐ not at all	☐ already ☐ not at all	☐ already ☐ not at all
4. I followed ____ of my teacher's directions.	☐ most or all ☐ some ☐ few or none	☐ most or all ☐ some ☐ few or none	☐ most or all ☐ some ☐ few or none
5. I understood the sentences ____.	☐ most of the time ☐ sometimes ☐ almost never	☐ most of the time ☐ sometimes ☐ almost never	☐ most of the time ☐ sometimes ☐ almost never
6. When I didn't understand, I ____.	☐ asked for help ☐ said nothing	☐ asked for help ☐ said nothing	☐ asked for help ☐ said nothing

© HMH Supplemental Publishers Inc.

NAME _____

CHECKLIST

Word	I've never heard of it.	I've heard of it.	I know what it means.
British	☐	☐	☐
colony	☐	☐	☐
protest	☐	☐	☐
Boston Tea Party	☐	☐	☐
declare	☐	☐	☐
independence	☐	☐	☐
march	☐	☐	☐
liberty	☐	☐	☐

Which word did you find most challenging?

_____

© HMH Supplemental Publishers Inc.

NAME

CHECKLIST

Word	I've never heard of it.	I've heard of it.	I know what it means.
pamphlet	☐	☐	☐
refuse	☐	☐	☐
troops	☐	☐	☐
revolution	☐	☐	☐
battle	☐	☐	☐
document	☐	☐	☐
constitution	☐	☐	☐
property	☐	☐	☐

Which word did you find most interesting?

© HMH Supplemental Publishers Inc.

NAME _____

MONITORING SPEAKING CHECKLIST

	Unit 1 "Good Advice"	Unit 2 "On Trial"	Unit 3 "A Special Bird"
1. When I speak in class, I usually use _____.	☐ one or two words ☐ phrases ☐ complete sentences	☐ one or two words ☐ phrases ☐ complete sentences	☐ one or two words ☐ phrases ☐ complete sentences
2. I understand instructions and can repeat them in _____.	☐ one or two words ☐ phrases ☐ complete sentences	☐ one or two words ☐ phrases ☐ complete sentences	☐ one or two words ☐ phrases ☐ complete sentences
3. If asked about a story, I can identify _____.	☐ the characters ☐ the setting ☐ the conflict or problem	☐ the characters ☐ the setting ☐ the conflict or problem	☐ the characters ☐ the setting ☐ the conflict or problem
4. I can give my opinion or ideas about a story in _____.	☐ one or two words ☐ a sentence ☐ a discussion	☐ one or two words ☐ a sentence ☐ a discussion	☐ one or two words ☐ a sentence ☐ a discussion
5. I can tell my feelings about a story in _____.	☐ one or two words ☐ a sentence ☐ a discussion	☐ one or two words ☐ a sentence ☐ a discussion	☐ one or two words ☐ a sentence ☐ a discussion

© HMH Supplemental Publishers Inc.

NAME ——————————————————————————

NARRATIVE RUBRIC: Historical Fiction

When you write a historical fiction narrative, check it against this rubric. Did you do all you can to make it better?   Yes ☐   No ☐

	The Harvest	Duncan's Model	Class Model	My Model
1.	Historical fiction is a type of narrative that is set in the past and drawn from history. The main characters tend to be fictional.			
2.	It is clear **when** and **where** the story takes place.			
3.	The story uses authentic details.			
4.	The story uses facts and details that may require research.			
5.	The story may use dialogue to make characters come alive.			
6.	The story reveals the characters through what they say and do.			
7.	The actions follow each other in a logical way.			
8.	The ending seems right for the story.			
9.	The grammar, spelling, and punctuation are correct.			

Score
3. Excellent   **2. Good**   **1. Needs work**

© HMH Supplemental Publishers Inc.

NAME _____

NARRATIVE SEQUENCE ORGANIZER

About "The Harvest"

Row 1: In this historical fiction narrative, three events occur during the same approximate time frame. Those events are summarized in the first row.

Row 2: The outcome of the three events in row 1 is summarized in this row.

Row 3: The final outcome is summarized in this row.

1 | Matt worries about harvesting his wheat before the British arrive. | Hungry British soldiers move toward the farmlands. | Lady Schuyler heads to the farmlands, too.

2 Lady Schuyler asks Matt to make a sacrifice for his country.

3 Matt agrees and sets wheat field on fire.

© HMH Supplemental Publishers Inc.

NAME _____

CAPITALIZE PROPER NOUNS

A proper noun begins with a capital letter. A proper noun is a particular person, place, thing, or idea.
My dog's name is Bing.

Sometimes, a proper noun contains more than one word. Only the important words are capitalized.
I live in the United States of America.

People's titles are capitalized, even when they are abbreviations.
That man is Mister Smith. I saw Dr. Clark.

An adjective that is formed from a proper noun is capitalized.
An American flag waved in the breeze.

Rewrite each sentence. Capitalize the proper nouns.

1. jamie wrote to dr. eileen cruz.

_____

2. The panda bear has a chinese name.

_____

3. I can see venus through my telescope.

_____

4. Watch out, katie!

_____

5. The king of sweden has a crown.

_____

© HMH Supplemental Publishers Inc.

NAME _____

EDITING FOR GRAMMAR, SPELLING, AND PUNCTUATION

See also pages 166 and 170.

A verb must agree with its subject.
I am tall. She is tall. We are best friends.

A subject pronoun can take the place of a subject noun.
My aunt is an inventor. She builds robots.
My aunt and uncle work hard. They build amazing things.

Listen to your teacher. Compare the first draft of the practice paragraph to the edited draft.

Mom promised me an adventure for my birthday. She told me to pack a bag. We (was) going on a camping trip. I could hardly wait to find out where we were going. Mom and my brother (milo) packed the car. (She) smiled at each other as they worked. They had a secret. We started driving. After a few hours, I saw a sign. "Welcome to Big Bend." Wow! I've always wanted to visit (big bend)! Black bears live there. Maybe I'll see one!

Mom promised me an adventure for my birthday. She told me to pack a bag. We were going on a camping trip. I could hardly wait to find out where we were going. Mom and my brother Milo packed the car. They smiled at each other as they worked. They had a secret. We started driving. After a few hours, I saw a sign. "Welcome to Big Bend." Wow! I've always wanted to visit Big Bend! Black bears live there. Maybe I'll see one!

© HMH Supplemental Publishers Inc.

NAME —————————————————————————————

READER'S LOG: "EARLY THUNDER"

BEFORE READING: PAIR AND SHARE

1. My class talked about the _____.

☐ title   ☐ illustrations   ☐ _____

2. I understood _____ of the discussion.

☐ most or all   ☐ some   ☐ little or none

DURING READING

3. What are the major events in the story?

_____

_____

_____

4. Is there anything in the story that you do not understand? Write it here:

_____

_____

AFTER READING: PAIR AND SHARE

5. Talk to your partner about anything in the story that you do not understand.

Now, my partner and I understand _____.

Me   ☐ a lot better.   ☐ a little better.   ☐ no better.

My partner ☐ a lot better.   ☐ a little better.   ☐ no better.

© HMH Supplemental Publishers Inc.

NAME _____

MATCH IT UP

Write the letter of the definition that matches each word.

1. _____ declare

   A to express strong disagreement with something

2. _____ British

   B a group of people who settle in a new land to live and work together

3. _____ liberty

   C the act of walking together as a group for a reason

4. _____ march

   D the people and things that come from Great Britain

5. _____ colony

   E the freedom to live as we want

6. _____ protest

   F to say out loud in front of others

© HMH Supplemental Publishers Inc.

NAME _____

UNSCRAMBLE THE WORDS

Unscramble each word to spell one of the words in the box. Write the word on the line under the scrambled word.

CONSTITUTION	TROOPS	PAMPHLET	PROPERTY
DOCUMENT	REFUSE	BATTLE	REVOLUTION

1. OSTROP (soldiers)

_____

2. ESREUF (say that you are not willing to do something)

_____

3. TIROUNVELO (when people fight to change their country's government)

_____

4. TETLAB (a fight between groups of people)

_____

5. MOCEDUNT (an official paper)

_____

6. LATHMEPP (a thin booklet that explains ideas or information)

_____

7. TINONCISTOUT (the written document of a government's laws or rules)

_____

8. REPOYTRP (the things you own)

_____

© HMH Supplemental Publishers Inc.

NAME _____

A. Definition of Noun?

Read the first sentence. Circle the letter of the answer that best completes the second sentence.

1. The word *girl* is a noun.
   This word names a _____.

   A person   **C** thing

   B place   **D** idea

2. The word *jar* is a noun.
   This word names a _____.

   A person   **C** thing

   B place   **D** animal

B. Subject Pronouns and *to be* verbs

Read the first sentence. Circle the letter of the answer that best completes the second sentence.

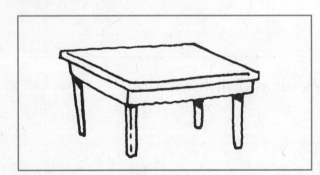

3. This is my table.
   _____ is very old.

   A She   **C** He

   B They   **D** It

4. Look at the dots.
   _____ are black.

   A They   **C** She

   B It   **D** I

© HMH Supplemental Publishers Inc.

NAME _____

5. Do you see the queen?
She _____ mad at the duck.

   A are   **C** is

   B am   **D** be

6. The dad has two kids.
They _____ all very happy.

   A are   **C** is

   B am   **D** be

PAIR AND SHARE With your partner, discuss: What is your favorite animal?

Use this sentence frame:

I like _____ the best!

Use plural nouns in your answers. Here is an example: *I like cats the best!*

Check pages 159–161 if you need help.

Monitor Language: How's your grammar?

Listen to your partner. Were the plural nouns correct?

Yes, always	Sometimes	Never
☐	☐	☐

How were your plural nouns? Were they correct?

Yes, always	Sometimes	Never
☐	☐	☐

© HMH Supplemental Publishers Inc.

NAME _____

CLOSE READING OF THE TEXT

 Self-monitor your understanding as you read.

1. **Reread**. Start with the last sentence you understood. Then read on from that point.

2. **Take notes**. Write down the most important details. This can help you understand and remember what you read.

3. **Look up words you don't know.**

4. **Ask questions**. Then look for answers to your questions in the text, or you can ask someone.

Personal Narrative	Notes
In Guatemala, I lived with my mom and dad. We lived on a farm. One day, a letter arrived. I could see that my parents were very happy and excited. I wondered what the letter was about, so I asked them. The letter said we would be able to move to the United States. My uncle lived in the U.S. He said *Mamá* and *Papá* could find good jobs there. We packed up our property and left.	Underline anything you do not understand. Take notes. What are the most important ideas? _____ _____ _____ Tell what you reread or a question you asked. _____ _____

© HMH Supplemental Publishers Inc.

NAME —————————————————————————

READ FOR RATE

Read the following passage aloud. Have a partner time your reading for one minute. Then, fill in the chart at the bottom of the page with the number of words you read. Read the passage a second and third time. Try to increase the number of words you read accurately in a minute.

Thomas Jefferson was born on April 13, 1743, in Virginia. He	11
is famous for writing the Declaration of Independence. In that	21
document, Jefferson wrote that all people are created equal.	30
He also wrote that all people have the right to be free.	42
Thomas Jefferson helped create the new government of	50
the United States. The government was defined in the	59
Constitution.	60
Thomas Jefferson was the third President of the United	69
States. He died on a very important day—July 4, 1826. That's	81
the same day the Declaration of Independence was signed	90
fifty years earlier.	93

Number of Words Read		
First Reading	Second Reading	Third Reading

© HMH Supplemental Publishers Inc.

NAME _____

CHECK YOUR UNDERSTANDING

A. Reread "from Early Thunder" on **Student Edition** pages 26–35. Then read each sentence below. Circle the letter of the correct answer.

1. Daniel and Beckett are looking for _____ to give Judge Ropes.

   A blankets   **C** sugar

   B medicine   **D** tea

2. The crowd of people outside the Judge's house are upset because _____.

   A Daniel and Beckett have taken some tea

   B the Judge's windows have been broken

   C they were woken up in the middle of the night

   D the Judge is very sick

© HMH Supplemental Publishers Inc.

NAME _____

B. Read each sentence below. Circle the letter of the correct answer.

3. Daniel knows the rumor about the Judge and the cat is false because _____.

   A the Judge would not deliberately spread smallpox

   B the Judge doesn't have a cat

   C Daniel is a friend of the Judge

   D both Daniel and the Judge are Tories

4. Daniel and Beckett plan to travel in the shadows in order to _____.

   A avoid being seen by the Liberty Boys

   B protect their tea

   C hide from their parents

   D take a shortcut

C. Read each question below. Circle the letter of the correct answer.

5. Why has the gang attacked the Judge's house?

   A They are celebrating the repeal of the stamp tax.

   B They are angry about some of the Judge's decisions.

   C They are angry because the Judge is a Tory.

   D They don't want to catch smallpox.

6. Why does Mrs. Foote want the Judge to know the town loves him?

   A She wants to show support for the Judge's political views.

   B She knows everyone there hates the Whigs and Patriots.

   C She thinks that will make him get better more quickly.

   D She wants him to know people care no matter what his political views.

© HMH Supplemental Publishers Inc.

NAME _____

A. Label

Write a word that names each picture. Use a word from the word box.

| egg | hat | jam | mop |
| lip | sax | sack | duck | zip |

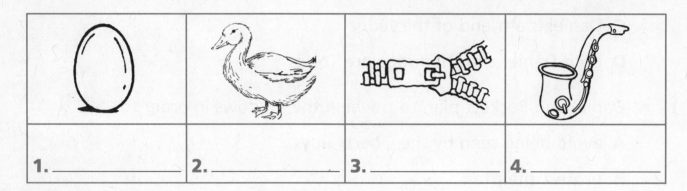

1. _____ 2. _____ 3. _____ 4. _____

B. Phonics

Read these words aloud. Use the phonics skills you have learned.

	A	B	C	D	E	F
5.	fan	Rex	it	not	up	no
6.	van	jet	quit	lot	sun	hi
7.	sat	egg	six	pop	fun	so
8.	has	yes	is	on	but	by
9.	mat	ten	zip	rock	cut	go
10.	gap	well	kill	sock	luck	my

C. High-Frequency Words

Read these words aloud.

| 11. | the | of | and | a | to | in |
| 12. | is | you | that | it | he | was |

© HMH Supplemental Publishers Inc.

NAME _____

D. Listen. Read. Check.

Your teacher will say a word. Mark the box next to the word.

13.	☐ me		☐ my		☐ hi
14.	☐ it		☐ hit		☐ at
15.	☐ fan		☐ fin		☐ fun
16.	☐ pit		☐ pet		☐ pot
17.	☐ sick		☐ sack		☐ sock
18.	☐ no		☐ not		☐ Nat
19.	☐ six		☐ sit		☐ sat
20.	☐ jet		☐ get		☐ Jed

E. Spelling

Your teacher will say a word. Write the word. Check your spelling.

21. _____   23. _____

22. _____   24. _____

© HMH Supplemental Publishers Inc.

NAME _____

CHECKLIST

Word	I've never heard of it.	I've heard of it.	I know what it means.
democracy	☐	☐	☐
rights	☐	☐	☐
political party	☐	☐	☐
government	☐	☐	☐
bill	☐	☐	☐
Congress	☐	☐	☐
veto	☐	☐	☐
represent	☐	☐	☐

Which word did you find most challenging?

_____

© HMH Supplemental Publishers Inc.

NAME _____

CHECKLIST

Word	I've never heard of it.	I've heard of it.	I know what it means.
executive branch	☐	☐	☐
judicial branch	☐	☐	☐
legislative branch	☐	☐	☐
checks and balances	☐	☐	☐
cooperate	☐	☐	☐
Supreme Court	☐	☐	☐
interpret	☐	☐	☐
justice	☐	☐	☐

Which word did you find most interesting?

_____

© HMH Supplemental Publishers Inc.

NAME _____

FRIENDLY LETTER RUBRIC

When you write a friendly letter, compare it to this rubric. Did you do all you can to make it better?   Yes ☐ No ☐

	Dear Daniella,	**María Elena's Model**	**Class Model**	**My Model**
1.	The letter is written in the first person, using *I* or *we*.			
2.	The letter has a date, a greeting, a body, and a closing.			
3.	The letter is written to communicate with a friend or relative.			
4.	The letter expresses the writer's thoughts and feelings.			
5.	The letter is readable and clearly written.			
6.	There are different kinds of sentences, and the sentences do not all start with the same word.			
7.	The grammar, spelling, and punctuation in the letter are correct.			

Score

3: Excellent   **2: Good**   **1. Needs work**

© HMH Supplemental Publishers Inc.

NAME —————————————————————————————

LETTER WRITING ORGANIZER

> ⓘ Who will receive the letter? ——————————————
> How would you describe the letter?
> ☐ Personal   ☐ School   ☐ Business

Check any that apply: **Circle examples:**

☐ thank you   for a speech, a gift, help

☐ invitation   to a party, to speak, to join a club

☐ description   of a gift, a new puppy, a storm

☐ news   game results, family news, a concert

☐ information   class trip, due date, request to parents, event

☐ excuse   dog ate my homework, illness, fell asleep

☐ events in sequence   first, second, then, finally

Explain in more detail.

———————————————————————————————

———————————————————————————————

———————————————————————————————

© HMH Supplemental Publishers Inc.

NAME _____

END PUNCTUATION

> ℹ **Every sentence needs punctuation at the end.**
>
> **.** A statement tells something or describes something. A statement ends with a period.
> *My cat is called Sprinkles.*
>
> **?** A question is a sentence that asks something. A question ends with a question mark.
> *Where do you live?*
>
> **!** An exclamation is a sentence full of excitement, urgency, or feeling. An exclamation ends with an exclamation point.
> *I am so happy!*
>
> **.** or **!** A command, or imperative, tells someone to do something. A command ends with a period or an exclamation point.
> *Stay away from that dog!*
> *Come to my house tomorrow.*

© HMH Supplemental Publishers Inc.

Write the correct end punctuation for each sentence.

1. How old are you_____

2. I am ten years old_____

3. What is that animal_____

4. It's a dangerous snake_____

5. Run for your life_____

6. Can you see the snake_____

7. It's gone_____

8. Let's go home_____

NAME _____

EDITING FOR GRAMMAR, SPELLING, AND PUNCTUATION

See also pages 159 and 170.

 Some plural words end in –s. Some end in –es.

turtle and *turtles*   *fox* and *foxes*

 A verb must agree with its subject. Read these examples using forms of the verb *to be*.

I am here.   *We are all here.*
You are here.   *You are all here.*
She is here.   *They are all here.*

Listen to your teacher. Compare the first draft of a practice paragraph to the edited draft.

First Draft

People is in charge of their own mouths! If you say something that gets you in trouble, you are the one to blame. People do not usually mean to hurt other people's feelinges. Even so, sometimes they are careless. Why It are the same thing with gossip. Someone might feel hurt. So, please think before you say something.

Edited Draft

People are in charge of their own mouths! If you say something that gets you in trouble, you are the one to blame. People do not usually mean to hurt other people's feelings. Even so, sometimes they are careless. Why? It's the same thing with gossip. Someone might feel hurt. So, please think before you say something.

© HMH Supplemental Publishers Inc.

NAME _____

READER'S LOG: "HOW OUR GOVERNMENT WORKS"

> ⓘ Active listeners pay close attention and make notes. Active readers do, too. Write only what you need to remember the most important information.

PAIR AND SHARE Reread the selection with your partner. Mark the boxes and take notes as you read. Add to your notes as you talk to your partner.

1. How difficult is the selection?

   ☐ very difficult   ☐ not too difficult   ☐ easy

2. What makes the selection difficult?

   ☐ the words   ☐ the information   ☐ everything!

3. List the most difficult words.

   _____

4. What did you do about the difficult words?

   ☐ We talked about them.   ☐ We looked at the pictures.

   ☐ We looked them up in a dictionary.   ☐ We asked our teacher.

5. How did you use the pictures and text boxes? Did they help you?

   _____

6. Are there any sentences that you don't understand?

   Note the page number, and ask your teacher what they mean. _____

© HMH Supplemental Publishers Inc.

NAME ———————————————————

WHICH WORD AM I?

Read the clues. Write the correct vocabulary word from the box to match each clue.

| bill   represent   rights   political party   veto   government |

1. I am a group of people in charge of a city, state, or country.

———————————————————————————————

2. I am the things we can do by law.

———————————————————————————————

3. I am the act of refusing to accept or allow something.

———————————————————————————————

4. I am the written draft for a new law.

———————————————————————————————

5. I am what people in Congress do when they speak for you and stand up for your rights.

———————————————————————————————

6. I am a group of people who share ideas about how government should work.

———————————————————————————————

© HMH Supplemental Publishers Inc.

NAME _____

WHICH WORD?

Write the vocabulary word from the box to complete each sentence.

| cooperate   interpret   checks and balances |
| legislative branch   justice   judicial branch |

1. In a system of _____, each branch should have the same amount of power as the others.

_____

2. If you _____ with someone, then you work together.

_____

3. The _____ writes and passes new laws.

_____

4. The _____ decides if laws are fair.

_____

5. If you _____ something, you decide what something means.

_____

6. _____ means fair treatment for all under the law.

_____

© HMH Supplemental Publishers Inc.

NAME ───────────────────────────────────

A. Subject Pronouns and *to be* Verbs

Circle the letter of the correct answer.

1. My sister and I work out.
We _____ strong.

   A was   **C** is

   B are   **D** were

2. Please sing more, Marissa!
_____ are a good singer!

   A He   **C** We

   B She   **D** You

3. Listen to me! Do what I say!
I _____ the king.

   A is   **C** am

   B are   **D** will

4. This is my city!
_____ is huge!

   A It   **C** We

   B She   **D** They

© HMH Supplemental Publishers Inc.

NAME

B. Combining Sentences

Write one new sentence that combines the information in the sentences above each picture.

The book is in my room.
The phone is in my room.

My dad cooks. My mom cooks.
I cook.

5. _____

_____.

6. _____

_____.

PAIR AND SHARE With your partner, discuss words you can use to describe yourselves. Use nouns and adjectives.

Use these sentence frames:

A. Nouns

I am a _____. (brother, boy, son)

You are a _____. (friend, student)

B. Adjectives

I am _____. (thin, tall, tired)

You are _____. (friendly, helpful)

Check page 164 to review adjectives. Make sure you use the correct verb form. See page 170 to review forms of *to be*.

Monitor Language: How's your grammar?

Listen to your partner. Were the nouns, adjectives, and verb forms correct?

Yes, always	Sometimes	Never
☐	☐	☐

How were your nouns, adjectives, and verb forms? Were they correct?

Yes, always	Sometimes	Never
☐	☐	☐

© HMH Supplemental Publishers Inc.

NAME _____

CLOSE READING OF THE TEXT

 Self-monitor your understanding as you read.

1. **Reread**. Start with the last sentences you understood. Then read on from that point.

2. **Take notes**. Write down the most important details. This can help you understand and remember what you read.

3. **Look up words you don't know.**

4. **Ask questions**. Then look for answers to your questions in the text, or you can ask someone.

Mystery	Notes
"Elena! Maybe you can help me solve a mystery," said the President. "I wrote an important letter to members of Congress. I have to stamp it with my official seal, but I can't find the seal anywhere," he explained. "It was on my desk this morning. Now it's gone! If I don't send this letter today, it could cost our country thirty million dollars. Can you help me, Elena?'"	Underline anything you do not understand. Take notes. What are the most important ideas? _____ _____ _____ Tell what you reread or a question you asked. _____ _____ _____

© HMH Supplemental Publishers Inc.

NAME _____

READ WITH EXPRESSION

Read the following poem aloud. Read with energy and strong emotion. Pause for punctuation marks such as commas and periods. Listen to your partner's reading. Then practice the passage a second time.

Note: One slash (/) indicates a short pause for a dash. Two slashes (//) indicates that you stop for a period, a question mark, or an exclamation point.

Freedom. //

Can you smell it? //

Can you taste it? //

Can you see it? //

Freedom is the air we breathe. //

It is the food we eat. //

It is the company we keep. //

It is the words in our mouths. //

It is the prayer we make. //

It is the privacy we stake. //

Our Bill of Rights lets us know

Just how far we can go. //

Ten rights that keep us free— /

You and me! //

© HMH Supplemental Publishers Inc.

NAME _____

CHECK YOUR UNDERSTANDING

A. Reread "Why Do We Have a Constitution?" on **Student Edition** pages 72–75. Then read each sentence below. Circle the letter of the correct answer.

1. Long ago, England was ruled by a _____.

    A president   **C** king

    B lord   **D** duke

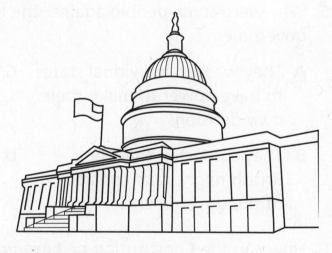

2. The highest law of the United States is the _____.

    A Constitution   **C** Articles of Confederation

    B Bill of Rights   **D** parliament

© HMH Supplemental Publishers Inc.

NAME _____

B. Read each question below. Circle the letter of the correct answer.

3. The representatives of the states wrote the Constitution in order to _____.

   A break away from England

   B create the rules for a government of the United States

   C make sure individual citizens had rights

   D set up a parliament like the one in England

4. The Constitution does NOT _____.

   A describe the positions in the United States government

   B explain how the government makes laws

   C have separate rules for each state

   D explain how office holders are chosen

C. Read each question below. Circle the letter of the correct answer.

5. Why were some people against the idea of a strong United States government?

   A They wanted individual states to have power to make their own decisions.

   B They suspected that the British might take control of the government.

   C They didn't believe in democracy.

   D They thought a central government would work.

6. How can the Constitution be kept up to date?

   A We can go back to using the Articles of Confederation.

   B Some parts of the Constitution can be ignored.

   C The people can write a new Constitution.

   D Amendments can be added to the Constitution.

© HMH Supplemental Publishers Inc.

NAME _____

A. Label.

Write a word that names each picture. Use a word from the box.

| bat | cub | boat | cube | ran | kit | rain | kite |

1. _____ 2. _____ 3. _____ 4. _____

B. Phonics

Read these words aloud. Use the phonics skills you have learned.

	A	B	C	D	E	F	G
5.	see	pane	kite	may	home	Eve	fume
6.	rain	tame	line	team	lone	Zeke	cube
7.	pay	safe	mile	coat	doze	Pete	tube
8.	toad	quake	pipe	keep	mole	beet	mute
9.	meat	tape	bite	pain	bone	peek	tune
10.	be	wade	hike	say	cope	feat	rude

C. High-Frequency Words

Read these words aloud.

11.	for	on	are	as	with	his
12.	they	I	at	be	this	have

© HMH Supplemental Publishers Inc.

NAME _____

D. Listen. Read. Check.

Your teacher will say a word. Mark the box next to the word.

13.	☐ quake		☐ cake		☐ quack
14.	☐ way		☐ wade		☐ wait
15.	☐ rain		☐ ray		☐ ran
16.	☐ cub		☐ cube		☐ cab
17.	☐ bit		☐ by		☐ bite
18.	☐ mutt		☐ mute		☐ muck
19.	☐ feed		☐ fed		☐ feet
20.	☐ pat		☐ pet		☐ Pete

E. Spelling

Your teacher will say a word. Write the word. Check your spelling.

21. _____   23. _____

22. _____   24. _____

© HMH Supplemental Publishers Inc.

NAME

CHECKLIST

Word	I've never heard of it.	I've heard of it.	I know what it means.
vibration	☐	☐	☐
eardrum	☐	☐	☐
sound waves	☐	☐	☐
beat	☐	☐	☐
note	☐	☐	☐
volume	☐	☐	☐
amplify	☐	☐	☐
muffle	☐	☐	☐

Which word did you find most challenging?

_____

© HMH Supplemental Publishers Inc.

NAME _____

CHECKLIST

Word	I've never heard of it.	I've heard of it.	I know what it means.
percussion instruments	☐	☐	☐
wind instruments	☐	☐	☐
string instruments	☐	☐	☐
brass instruments	☐	☐	☐
pitch	☐	☐	☐
reflect	☐	☐	☐
detect	☐	☐	☐
echo	☐	☐	☐

Which word did you find most interesting?

_____

© HMH Supplemental Publishers Inc.

NAME —————————————————————————————————————

READING LONGER WORDS

 Reading Closed Syllables When a word or syllable has one vowel and ends in a consonant, the vowel usually stands for a *short* vowel sound.

 You can divide:

- between the words in a compound word.
- after a prefix, or before a suffix.
- between the consonants in a VCCV letter pattern.

A. Draw a slash (/) between the two words. Read the smaller words. Then read the compound word.

c a n n o t	s u n s e t	b a c k p a c k

B. Draw a slash (/) between the two word parts. Read the word parts. Then read the compound word.

u n l i t	u n p a c k	d i s m i s s

C. In longer words, look for a VCCV letter pattern (a vowel plus two consonants plus another vowel).

u p s e t	n a p k i n	f a b r i c

D. Use the strategies you have learned to divide the words. Read each part. Then read the whole word.

c a c t u s	p a d l o c k	p u b l i c

© HMH Supplemental Publishers Inc.

NAME _____

PERSONAL NARRATIVE

When you write a personal narrative, compare it to this rubric. Did you do all you can to make it better? Yes ☐ No ☐

	The Lesson	Sabrina's Model	Class Model	My Model
1.	It is told in the first person, using *I* or *we*.			
2.	It uses dialogue to make characters come alive.			
3.	The story reveals the characters through what they do and say.			
4.	The actions follow each other in a way that makes sense.			
5.	Words help explain the order.			
6.	It is clear **when** and **where** the story takes place.			
7.	The ending is good! It seems right for the story!			
8.	The grammar, spelling, and punctuation are correct.			
9.	Readers will like the story!			

Score

3. Excellent   **2.** Good   **1.** Needs work

© HMH Supplemental Publishers Inc.

NAME

PERSONAL NARRATIVE SEQUENCE ORGANIZER

1. Sabrina, the girl telling the story, loves to play music on the piano.

2. Sabrina practices nonstop to get ready for a big, important audition.

3. Sabrina loses the competition.

4. She is very disappointed so she quits piano lessons.

5. She agrees to give lessons to a young boy.

6. Music becomes a happy part of her life again.

© HMH Supplemental Publishers Inc.

NAME _____

COMMAS IN A LIST

 Commas separate objects or phrases in a list.

> , If there are more than two things in a list, use a comma between them.
> *We play with baseballs, footballs, and soccer balls.*
>
> Do not use a comma when there are only two things in the list.
> *We play with baseballs and footballs.*
>
> , Put a comma between phrases in a list.
> *The dog looked on the bed, under the bed, and in its basket.*

Rewrite each sentence, using the correct punctuation.

1. We carried a basket a blanket and a football to the park.

_____

2. The park has a pond tables and fields.

_____

3. Ducks in the pond quacked flapped their wings and paddled.

_____

4. Jason and Lee were also at the park.

_____

5. We looked in the car in the basket and in our pockets.

_____

© HMH Supplemental Publishers Inc.

NAME

EDITING FOR GRAMMAR, SPELLING, AND PUNCTUATION

See also pages 173 and 174.

 The present tense of a verb describes an action that is happening now.
The horses walk down the street.

 The past tense of a verb describes action that happened in the past.
The horses walked down the street.

 An adverb often describes a verb. It usually ends in –*ly*.
Incorrect: *The drums beat loud.*
Correct: *The drums beat loudly.*

Listen to your teacher. Compare the first draft of a poem to the edited draft.

First Draft	Edited Draft
Listen to the wind. It tells a story,	Listen to the wind. It tells a story,
When it rustles through Autumn's leaves.	When it rustles through Autumn's leaves.
It whispered of a winter worry.	It whispers of a winter worry.
Mouse scampers quick among the trees.	Mouse scampers quickly among the trees.
"Where is it?" he asks. "I'm in a hurry	"Where is it?" he asks. "I'm in a hurry
To find a hole to make my nest,	To find a hole to make my nest,
a place to climb inside and rest,	A place to climb inside and rest,
And hide from Winter's coldest blast. Brrrr!"	And hide from Winter's coldest blast. Brrrr!"

© HMH Supplemental Publishers Inc.

NAME _____

READER'S LOG: "THE LOVELIEST SONG OF ALL"

BEFORE READING: PAIR AND SHARE

1. My class talked about the _____.

☐ title   ☐ illustrations   ☐ _____

2. I understood _____ of the discussion.

☐ most or all   ☐ some   ☐ little or none

DURING READING

3. What are the major events in the story?

_____

_____

_____

4. Is there anything in the story that you do not understand? Write it here:

_____

_____

AFTER READING: PAIR AND SHARE

5. Talk to your partner about anything in the story that you do not understand.

Now, my partner and I understand _____.

Me   ☐ a lot better   ☐ a little better   ☐ no better

My partner   ☐ a lot better   ☐ a little better   ☐ no better

© HMH Supplemental Publishers Inc.

NAME ————————————————————————————————

MATCH IT UP

Write the letter of the definition that matches each word.

1. _____ amplify

    A to make a sound quieter

2. _____ note

    B vibrations that travel through the air

3. _____ volume

    C to make something sound louder or stronger

4. _____ muffle

    D the amount of sound made by a musical instrument, voice, radio, TV, or CD player

5. _____ sound waves

    E a thin layer of skin between the outer ear and inner ear

6. _____ eardrum

    F a single sound of music

© HMH Supplemental Publishers Inc.

NAME _____

USE CLUES

Read each sentence. Use context clues to help you figure out the correct vocabulary word from the box to complete each sentence. Write the word on the line.

brass instruments	detect	percussion instrument
pitch	string instruments	echo

1. Uncle Jorge says that his favorite _____ are the violin and the cello.

_____

2. Inside a cave, you can hear the _____ of your voice bouncing off the rock walls.

_____

3. Bats can make a noise that has such a high _____ that humans can't hear it.

_____

4. Natalie wanted to learn a _____, so her parents got her a drum.

_____

5. When I walked into my house, I could _____ the sound of voices in the kitchen.

_____

6. Many jazz musicians play _____, such as the trombone and the trumpet.

_____

© HMH Supplemental Publishers Inc.

NAME _____

A. Action Verbs: Present Tense

Circle the letter of the correct answer.

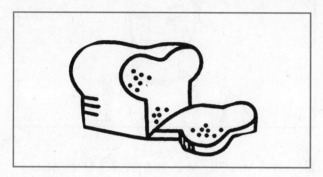

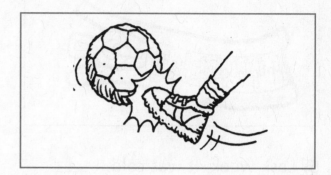

1. I like bread a lot. Juan _____ it a lot, too.

   A like   C liking

   B likes   D liked

2. Dan kicks the ball. Marta kicks the ball. We all _____ the ball.

   A kicks   C kick

   B licking   D were

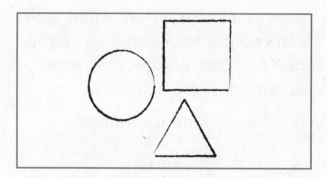

3. Look at the ducks! They _____ all the time.

   A quack   C quacking

   B quacks   D are

4. I see the shapes. Kim _____ the shapes too.

   A sees   C seeing

   B see   D is

© HMH Supplemental Publishers Inc.

NAME _____

B. Action Verbs: Past Tense

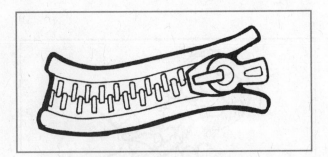

5. Lask week, it was cold. I _____ up my coat to the top.

   A zip   **C** zipped

   B zipping   **D** zipper

6. Last week, we went to the zoo. Roberto _____ all day.

   A smiles   **C** smiling

   B smiled   **D** will smile

PAIR AND SHARE With your partner, discuss how you spend your weekends. What action verbs can you use to describe what you do? Ask your partner questions about her or his activities.

Use these sentence frames:

A. Tell about yourself.

On the weekend, I usually _____. (run, play, study, sleep)

B. Tell about what a family member or friend does on weekends.

On the weekend, my dad usually _____. (plays chess, watches TV, reads books)

Check page 173 to review action verbs. Make sure you use the correct verb form.

Monitor Language: How's your grammar?

Listen to your partner. Were the verb forms correct?

Yes, always	Sometimes	Never
☐	☐	☐

How were your verb forms? Were they correct?

Yes, always	Sometimes	Never
☐	☐	☐

© HMH Supplemental Publishers Inc.

NAME _____

CLOSE READING OF THE TEXT

 Self-monitor your understanding as you read.

1. **Reread.** Start with the last sentence you understood. Then read on from that point.

2. **Take notes.** Write down the most important details. This can help you understand and remember what you read.

3. **Look up words you don't know.**

4. **Ask questions.** Then look for answers to your questions in the text, or you can ask someone.

Observation Log	Notes
First, I listened to how the noise sounded when it traveled through air. It was loud. Second, I put my radio under a pile of foam pillows. I could hardly hear the music. The music was muffled. Next, I wrapped the radio in wool blankets. I put my ear against the blankets. The sound was very muffled. Finally, I put the radio on a wooden table. I put my ear against the table. The sound was clear.	Underline anything you do not understand. Take notes. What are the most important ideas? _____ _____ _____ Tell what you reread or a question you asked. _____ _____ _____

© HMH Supplemental Publishers Inc.

© HMH Supplemental Publishers Inc.

NAME _____

READ FOR ACCURACY

Work with a partner. Take turns reading the passage aloud. As you read, concentrate on pronouncing each word correctly and speaking clearly. Then review the passage together. Write the difficult words on the lines below. Practice saying the words aloud. Then read the passage a second time.

> Ocean water is sometimes hard to see through. So dolphins send out clicks and creaking vibrations that have a high pitch. The sounds reflect off objects in the water. Returning echoes tell the dolphins if something is nearby. This is called echolocation.
>
> Bats use echolocation, too. Their big ears are constantly moving. They detect and amplify the buzz of a bug. Then the bat can send out sounds, listen for their echoes, and fly to the right place for an insect snack!

NAME ————————————————————————————

CHECK YOUR UNDERSTANDING

A. Reread "The Loveliest Song of All" on **Student Edition** pages 118–123. Then read each sentence below. Circle the letter of the correct answer.

1. The king calls his advisors because _____.

   A the princess is sad

   B the princess must marry

   C they must bring the princess gifts

   D they must entertain the princess

2. At first, the simply dressed man gets the princess's attention by _____.

   A playing games with her

   B talking about his village

   C singing beautifully

   D giving her jewels and money

© HMH Supplemental Publishers Inc.

NAME _____

B. Read each sentence below. Circle the letter of the correct answer.

3. The young man promises the princess that he will _____.

   A teach her to make a wind instrument

   B learn to sing like the birds in three full moons

   C make her happy

   D dance for her

4. The Spirit of the Woods helps the young man by _____.

   A teaching the young man a beautiful song

   B telling the princess to marry the young man

   C making a musical instrument that the young man can play

   D playing different musical notes

C. Read each question below. Circle the letter of the correct answer.

5. What is a *chirimía*?

   A a kind of music that is played in the forest

   B a joyful dance

   C a musical instrument that is played by blowing through one end

   D a bird that has colorful feathers

6. Why does the princess decide to marry the young man?

   A He plays a song that is even more beautiful than the birds' songs, and it makes her happy.

   B The king tells the princess that she must marry the young man.

   C The princess must marry after three moons have passed.

   D The Spirit of the Woods convinces the princess to marry the young man.

© HMH Supplemental Publishers Inc.

NAME _____

A. Label

Write a word that names each picture. Use a word from the word box.

pad	page	ship	chip	bath	shapes
	cent		sell		

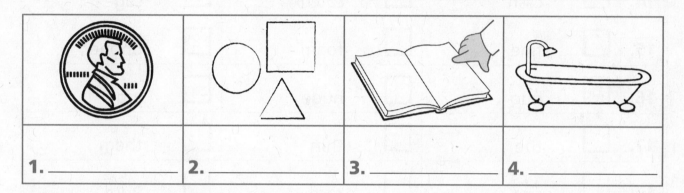

1. _____ 2. _____ 3. _____ 4. _____

B. Phonics

Read these words aloud. Use the phonics skills you have learned.

	A	B	C	D	E	F	G
5.	ship	sheet	path	thus	ace	game	gem
6.	chip	leash	thin	then	cage	coal	cell
7.	cash	wheel	math	that	mice	goal	gel
8.	rich	phone	with	them	huge	cope	cent
9.	rash	whee	thick	than	race	gain	gene
10.	catch	cheap	bath	this	wage	cone	cease

C. High-Frequency Words

Read these words aloud.

11.	from	or	one	had	by	word
12.	but	not	what	all	were	we

© HMH Supplemental Publishers Inc.

NAME _____

D. Listen. Read. Check.

Your teacher will say a word. Mark the box next to the word.

13.	☐ rash		☐ rich		☐ chip
14.	☐ cash		☐ catch		☐ cage
15.	☐ fine		☐ foam		☐ phone
16.	☐ hug		☐ huge		☐ jug
17.	☐ the		☐ thin		☐ them
18.	☐ rice		☐ race		☐ Russ
19.	☐ whip		☐ wipe		☐ hip
20.	☐ age		☐ jay		☐ gem

E. Spelling

Your teacher will say a word. Write the word. Check your spelling.

21. _____   23. _____

22. _____   24. _____

© HMH Supplemental Publishers Inc.

NAME —————————————————————————

MONITORING LISTENING CHECKLIST

> (i) Active listeners take notes. Don't try to write everything. Just note what you need in order to remember the most important information.

	Unit 4 In the Deep	Unit 5 A Growing Nation	Unit 6 Technology Matters!
1. What is the topic?			
2. The general meaning of the discussion was ____.			
3. I knew most of the words ____.	☐ already ☐ not at all	☐ already ☐ not at all	☐ already ☐ not at all
4. I understood the sentences ____.	☐ most of the time ☐ sometimes ☐ almost never	☐ most of the time ☐ sometimes ☐ almost never	☐ most of the time ☐ sometimes ☐ almost never
5. The main point of the topic is now ____.	☐ very clear ☐ a little clearer ☐ still confusing	☐ very clear ☐ a little clearer ☐ still confusing	☐ very clear ☐ a little clearer ☐ still confusing
6. My notes helped me understand the discussion ____.	☐ a lot ☐ a little ☐ not at all	☐ a lot ☐ a little ☐ not at all	☐ a lot ☐ a little ☐ not at all

© HMH Supplemental Publishers Inc.

NAME _____

CHECKLIST

Word	I've never heard of it.	I've heard of it.	I know what it means.
environment	☐	☐	☐
organism	☐	☐	☐
zone	☐	☐	☐
depth	☐	☐	☐
trench	☐	☐	☐
coral	☐	☐	☐
marine	☐	☐	☐
exist	☐	☐	☐

Which word did you find most challenging?

_____

© HMH Supplemental Publishers Inc.

NAME

CHECKLIST

Word	I've never heard of it.	I've heard of it.	I know what it means.
transparent	☐	☐	☐
bacteria	☐	☐	☐
life form	☐	☐	☐
survive	☐	☐	☐
seaweed	☐	☐	☐
surround	☐	☐	☐
salt water	☐	☐	☐
surface	☐	☐	☐

Which word did you find most interesting?

_____

© HMH Supplemental Publishers Inc.

NAME _____

MONITORING SPEAKING CHECKLIST

	Unit 4 "Taking Care of Lola"	Unit 5 "Basketball Stories"	Unit 6 "Whose Phone?"
1. I can describe the characters and setting in ____.	☐ one or two words ☐ phrases ☐ complete sentences	☐ one or two words ☐ phrases ☐ complete sentences	☐ one or two words ☐ phrases ☐ complete sentences
2. I can retell the story in ____.	☐ a complete way ☐ a sentence ☐ a word or two	☐ a complete way ☐ a sentence ☐ a word or two	☐ a complete way ☐ a sentence ☐ a word or two
3. I explain my opinions and ideas about the story in a way that others ____.	☐ often agree with ☐ understand ☐ do not understand	☐ often agree with ☐ understand ☐ do not understand	☐ often agree with ☐ understand ☐ do not understand
4. My speaking skills are ____.	☐ improving ☐ staying the same	☐ improving ☐ staying the same	☐ improving ☐ staying the same

© HMH Supplemental Publishers Inc.

NAME ———————————————————————————————

READING LONGER WORDS

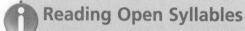 **Reading Open Syllables**

When a word or syllable ends in a vowel, the vowel usually stands for a *long* vowel sound.

When you see a VCV letter pattern, first try dividing the word before the consonant. Read the word using a long vowel sound for the open syllable. (Example: p h o / t o) If the word doesn't sound quite right, try dividing after the consonant. Then read the word again, using a short vowel sound. (Example: p a n / i c)

A. Divide the word *before* the consonant in the VCV letter pattern. Read each syllable. Then read the whole word.

photo	ego	logo	pupil

B. Divide the word. Find the VCV letter pattern. Read each syllable. Then read the whole word.

begin	robot	cubic	music

C. Divide the word. Find the VCV letter pattern. Read each syllable. Then read the whole word.

panic	comic	rapid	robin

D. Divide the word. Find the VCV letter pattern. Read each syllable. Then read the whole word.

siren	recess	denim	humid
comet	finish	open	visit

© HMH Supplemental Publishers Inc.

NAME _____

OPINION RUBRIC

When you write a report that states an opinion, check it against this rubric.

Did you do all you can to make your position convincing? Yes ☐   No ☐

	Save Our Sea Turtles!	Rufaro's Model	Class Model	My Model
1.	The title hints at the topic and the writer's opinion about it.			
2.	The writer's opinion is stated at the beginning of the report.			
3.	Facts and examples support the writer's opinion.			
4.	Facts and examples are important and convincing.			
5.	It is clear what the writer wants the reader to do.			
6.	The opinion report is neat and easy to read.			
7.	The sentences are varied in length.			
8.	The grammar, spelling, and punctuation are correct.			
9.	Readers will get involved with this opinion and take a stand!			

Score

3. Excellent   2. Good   1. Needs work

© HMH Supplemental Publishers Inc.

NAME _____

OPINION REPORT ORGANIZER

The purpose of an opinion report is to convince the reader to agree with you and to take some kind of action. Follow these steps when you write your opinion.

1. Identify your **topic.** (You can hint at it in the title.)

2. State your **opinion** clearly in the introduction.

3. Identify **facts** that support your opinion.

4. Identify any possible **argument against** your opinion.

5. Tell readers what they should do. That's your **call to action!**

My topic: _____

My opinion: _____

_____

Facts that support my opinion:

- _____

- _____

- _____

Argument against my opinion: _____

Call to action: _____

_____

© HMH Supplemental Publishers Inc.

© HMH Supplemental Publishers Inc.

NAME _____

END PUNCTUATION

> ⓘ **Every sentence needs punctuation at the end.**
>
> **.** A statement tells something or describes something.
> A statement ends with a period.
> *The blue sky was filled with fluffy clouds.*
>
> **?** A question asks something. A question ends with a question mark.
> *What would you like to do today?*
>
> **!** An exclamation expresses excitement, the need to act, or a feeling. An exclamation ends with an exclamation point.
> *I am afraid of spiders!*
>
> **.** or **!** A command, or imperative, tells someone to do something. A command ends with a period or an exclamation point.
> *Take two steps forward. Don't go near the cliff!*

Add the correct punctuation at the end of each sentence.

1. Whales are some of the largest animals on the planet_____

2. Killer whales can grow to be twenty-eight feet long_____

3. Did you know that fin whales can be up to 88 feet long_____

4. Listen to the killer whale's whistle_____

5. What sound does the fin whale make_____

6. All whales communicate by making sounds in the water_____

7. Look out _____ There's a shark over there_____

8. I'm excited about visiting the aquarium_____

NAME

EDITING FOR GRAMMAR, SPELLING, AND PUNCTUATION

See also pages 170 and 172.

(i) A contraction is two words put together to make one word. An apostrophe takes the place of the missing letter or letters.

I am ⇒ I'm   you are ⇒ you're
she is ⇒ she's   he is ⇒ he's   it is ⇒ it's
we are ⇒ we're   they are ⇒ they're

(i) A negative contraction combines a verb with the word *not*.

is not ⇒ isn't   are not ⇒ aren't
was not ⇒ wasn't   were not ⇒ weren't
does not ⇒ doesn't   will not ⇒ won't

Listen to your teacher. Compare the first draft of the practice paragraph to the edited draft.

Today, I observed my dogs in the backyard. Lily chased her tail for two full minutes₍She got excited when a squirrel ran along the fence. She barked wildly as she jumped and twisted in the air. (Shes) a natural acrobat. Toby (isnt.) He (doesnt) move unless he has to. He lay in the sun with his eyes closed. Both dogs enjoyed being outdoors, but they enjoyed themselves (different.)

Today, I observed my dogs in the backyard. Lily chased her tail for two full minutes! She got excited when a squirrel ran along the fence. She barked wildly as she jumped and twisted in the air. She's a natural acrobat. Toby isn't. He doesn't move unless he has to. He lay in the sun with his eyes closed. Both dogs enjoyed being outdoors, but they enjoyed themselves differently.

© HMH Supplemental Publishers Inc.

NAME _____

READER'S LOG: "LIFE DEEP DOWN"

ℹ️ Active listeners take notes. Active readers do, too. Write only
what you need to remember the most important information.

PAIR AND SHARE Reread the selection with your partner. Mark the boxes
and take notes as you read. Add to your notes as you talk to your partner.

1. How difficult is the selection?

☐ very difficult   ☐ not too difficult   ☐ easy

2. What makes the selection difficult?

☐ the words   ☐ the information   ☐ everything!

3. List the difficult words.

_____

4. What did you do about those words?

☐ We talked about them.   ☐ We looked them up in a dictionary.

☐ We looked at the pictures.   ☐ We asked our teacher.

5. What did you learn from the pictures? Did they help you?

_____

6. Are there any sentences that you don't understand?
Note the page number, and ask your teacher what they mean. _____

© HMH Supplemental Publishers Inc.

NAME _____

USE CLUES

Read each sentence. Use context clues to help you figure out the correct vocabulary word from the box to complete each sentence. Write the word on the line.

coral	environment	marine	trench
	depth	zone	

1. Orchids grow well in the hot and humid _____ of the rain forest, but cactuses grow better in a dry place.

_____

2. My brother dug a long, deep _____ in the garden, and he planted a row of beans in it.

_____

3. Angelfish, sharks, and jellyfish are some of the _____ animals that can be found in the Atlantic Ocean.

_____

4. People in Texas are in a different time _____ from people in California.

_____

5. The deepest part of the Pacific Ocean has a _____ of over 11,000 feet.

_____

6. The _____ reef near Florida is made from the bones of millions of small sea animals.

_____

© HMH Supplemental Publishers Inc.

NAME _____

WHICH WORD?

Write the vocabulary word from the box to complete each sentence.

survive	transparent	surface	seaweed
	surrounds	life form	

1. When you _____, you stay alive even if it is difficult.

_____

2. If something _____ you, it is all around you.

_____

3. If something is _____, it is clear and you can see through it.

_____

4. A _____ is a living thing, such as a plant or an animal.

_____

5. The _____ is the outside or the top of something.

_____

6. All kinds of _____ are plants that grow in the ocean.

_____

© HMH Supplemental Publishers Inc.

NAME

Using Contractions with *to be* and *not*

Read each question. Circle the letter of the sentence that answers it.

1. Is that Dad's box?

  A Yes, it's his box.

  B Yes, they are.

  C Yes, we can.

2. Is that a drum?

  A Yes, it's a drum.

  B No, it isn't a drum.

  C It wasn't fun.

3. Are the kids pals?

  A No, it isn't.

  B He is a pal.

  C Yes, they're pals.

4. Are you kids all on the bus?

  A Yes, we're on it.

  B No, I'm not.

  C No, he isn't.

5. Is that a bell?

  A No, it isn't.

  B Yes, it's a bell.

  C You're a bell.

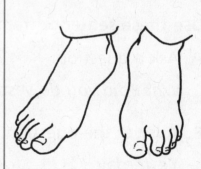

6. Are your feet sore?

  A Yes, they're feet.

  B No, I'm not.

  C Yes, they're sore.

© HMH Supplemental Publishers Inc.

NAME _____

7. Is it raining?

   A No, it isn't raining.

   B Yes, it's raining.

   C We're not wet.

8. Is that a fish?

   A No, I'm not.

   B Yes, it's a fish.

   C No, it isn't a fish.

PAIR AND SHARE With your partner, discuss what you did yesterday.

Use these sentence frames:

A. Ask a question.

   What did you do yesterday?

B. Answer the question.

   Yesterday, I _____. (cleaned my room, watched TV, finished my math)

Check page 174 to review the past-tense forms of action verbs. Make sure you use the correct verb form.

Monitor Language: How's your grammar?

Listen to your partner. Were the past-tense verb forms correct?

Yes, always	Sometimes	Never
☐	☐	☐

How were your verb forms? Were they correct?

Yes, always	Sometimes	Never
☐	☐	☐

© HMH Supplemental Publishers Inc.

NAME

CLOSE READING OF THE TEXT

 Self-monitor your understanding as you read.

1. **Reread.** Start with the last sentences you understood. Then read on from that point.

2. **Take notes.** Write down the most important details. This can help you understand and remember what you read.

3. **Look up words you don't know.**

4. **Ask questions.** Then look for answers to your questions in the text, or you can ask someone.

Fiction	Notes
Ana and Donato looked out at the ocean. It was now even darker around them, but they could see what looked like a shipwreck. Seaweed grew on and around the wreck. Pieces of the ship were gone, and fish swam through the holes. "Look at those little fish! They seem to like the shipwreck," Ana said. Suddenly something moved. "There's one that's not so little! Look out!" Donato cried. But as the long fish neared the ship, it turned away.	Underline anything you do not understand. Take notes. What are the most important ideas?
	Tell what you reread or a question you asked.

© HMH Supplemental Publishers Inc.

NAME _____

READ FOR RATE

Read the following passage aloud. Have a partner time your reading for one minute. Then, fill in the chart at the bottom of the page with the number of words you read. Read the passage a second and third time. Try to increase the number of words you read accurately in a minute.

In 1977, two scientists went down in the Pacific Ocean in	11
ALVIN, a submarine designed to go deep in the ocean. They	22
were surprised to find many life forms in the deep-sea	33
environment. They even found creatures that glow in the	42
dark!	43
Some life that they found was centered around cracks in the	54
ocean floor called hydrothermal vents. The vents are full of a	65
chemical that is poisonous to most sea life. However, the	75
chemical doesn't kill the marine animals that live near the	85
vents. It helps them survive so they can reproduce.	94
The most surprising find was bacteria, the smallest living	103
organisms. Some of the bacteria use the chemical in the vents	114
to make their own food. These bacteria are the first link in the	127
food chain around the vents.	132

Number of Words Read		
First Reading	Second Reading	Third Reading

© HMH Supplemental Publishers Inc.

NAME _____

CHECK YOUR UNDERSTANDING

A. Reread "Life Deep Down" on Student Edition pages 166–171. Then read each sentence below. Circle the letter of the correct answer.

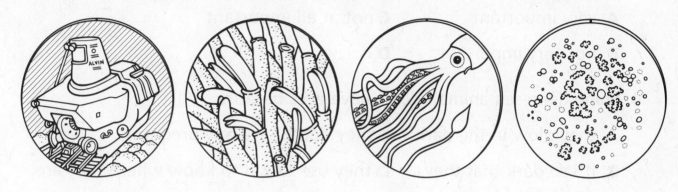

1. The smallest living organisms are _____.

  A ALVIN   **C** squid

  B tubeworms   **D** bacteria

2. Octopuses squirt ink so they can _____.

  A hide from predators   **C** see in the dark

  B attract fish to eat   **D** move faster

© HMH Supplemental Publishers Inc.

NAME _____

B. Read each sentence below. Circle the letter of the correct answer.

3. Animals have adapted to the deep-sea environment in amazing and unusual ways. This is a _____ idea in "Life Deep Down."

   A very important   C not at all important

   B not very important   D crazy

4. Some deep-sea animals don't have eyes because _____.

   A they glow in the dark   C they don't have any predators

   B it's so dark that they   D they use sound to know where they are
   don't need to see

C. Read each question below. Circle the letter of the correct answer.

5. Which information is interesting but not important to the text?

   A Deep-sea animals have adapted to living without sunlight.

   B The bacteria near the thermal vents make their own food from chemicals, not sunlight.

   C Deep-sea life forms are different from life near the surface.

   D Some squid are 60 feet long.

6. Why were the scientists surprised when they first traveled to the deep sea in ALVIN?

   A They thought they would crash, but they did not.

   B They did not expect to see so many deep-sea predators.

   C They thought the deep sea was too dark for plants or animals to live there, but they found many life forms.

   D They thought there would be sunlight, but it was almost completely dark.

© HMH Supplemental Publishers Inc.

NAME _____

A. Label

Write a word that names each picture. Use a word from the word box.

| bank | back | king | kick | him | hand | hats | jets |

1. _____
2. _____
3. _____
4. _____

B. Phonics

Read these words aloud. Use the phonics skills you have learned.

	A	B	C	D	E	F	G
5.	skin	last	bank	toe	flip	baby	rapid
6.	stitch	mask	bang	tie	brain	logo	habit
7.	spoke	toast	sunk	foe	clap	total	timid
8.	snack	list	thing	dye	band	icon	valid
9.	smell	risk	rung	Joe	melt	veto	limit
10.	slide	gasp	think	woe	tree	minus	denim

C. High-Frequency Words

Read these words aloud.

11.	when	your	can	said	there	use
12.	an	each	which	she	do	how

© HMH Supplemental Publishers Inc.

NAME _____

D. Listen. Read. Check.

Your teacher will say a word. Mark the box next to the word.

13.	☐ laid	☐ lad	☐ lady
14.	☐ cave	☐ cabinet	☐ cabin
15.	☐ sell	☐ smell	☐ melts
16.	☐ ask	☐ ax	☐ sax
17.	☐ rink	☐ ring	☐ Rick
18.	☐ sank	☐ sang	☐ sand
19.	☐ time	☐ tide	☐ tie
20.	☐ toad	☐ toe	☐ to

E. Spelling

Your teacher will say a word. Write the word. Check your spelling.

21._____   23._____

22._____   24._____

© HMH Supplemental Publishers Inc.

NAME

CHECKLIST

Word	I've never heard of it.	I've heard of it.	I know what it means.
westward expansion	☐	☐	☐
frontier	☐	☐	☐
wagon	☐	☐	☐
expedition	☐	☐	☐
journey	☐	☐	☐
caravan	☐	☐	☐
pioneer	☐	☐	☐
hardship	☐	☐	☐

Which word did you find most challenging?

© HMH Supplemental Publishers Inc.

NAME

CHECKLIST

Word	I've never heard of it.	I've heard of it.	I know what it means.
guide	☐	☐	☐
govern	☐	☐	☐
mission	☐	☐	☐
historic	☐	☐	☐
steamboat	☐	☐	☐
depend	☐	☐	☐
stagecoach	☐	☐	☐
camp	☐	☐	☐

Which word did you find most interesting?

_____

© HMH Supplemental Publishers Inc.

NAME

READING LONGER WORDS

ℹ️ **Reading Syllables with a VCe Letter Pattern**

Read these words: *hope, bike, Pete, same, cube.* They all have a vowel + a consonant + silent e. Look for this letter pattern in longer words.

ℹ️ You can divide:

- between the words in a compound word.
- after a prefix, or before a suffix.
- between the consonants in a VCCV letter pattern.
- before or after the consonant in a VCV letter pattern.

A. Divide the word. Circle the VCe letter pattern. Read each syllable. Then read the whole word.

erase	unite	locate
donate	refine	reuse

B. Divide the word. Circle the VCe letter pattern. Read each syllable. Then read the whole word.

inflate	dislike	mistake	exhale

C. Divide the word. Circle the VCe letter pattern. Read each syllable. Then read the whole word.

divide	decade	volume

D. Divide the word. Circle the VCe letter pattern. Read each syllable. Then read the whole word.

reptile	confuse	invite	escape
update	bedtime	online	inside

© HMH Supplemental Publishers Inc.

NAME _____

REPORT RUBRIC: Compare and Contrast

When you write a report, check it against this rubric.

Did you do everything you can to make it better?   Yes ☐   No ☐

	Survival!	Roberto's Model	Class Model	My Model
1.	The facts are correct. (Should you check the information again?)			
2.	Identify what you are comparing and contrasting.			
3.	It is clear how the two topics are alike.			
4.	It is clear how the two topics are different.			
5.	There is a summary at the end of the report.			
6.	The grammar, spelling, and punctuation are correct.			
7.	Readers will find the report interesting.			

Score

3. Excellent   2. Good   1. Needs work

© HMH Supplemental Publishers Inc.

NAME ——————————————————————————————————

REPORT ORGANIZER: Compare and Contrast

Before you write a report, create an organizer to help you make a plan.

What is Compared?	Same or different?	Explanation
Country of origin	Same	Both from England
Motivation	Same	Both seeking new opportunities to change their lives
	Different	**Massachusetts Bay:** sought freedom to practice Puritan religion **Jamestown:** seeking riches
Ready for hardships	Same	Neither group was prepared for hardships
Future Plans	Different	**Jamestown:** get rich and return to England **Massachusetts Bay:** wanted to practice their religion, work hard, stay in America
Relationships with Native People	Different	**Massachusetts Bay Colony** wanted peace and harmony with Native populations **Jamestown** colonists wanted to dominate and exploit the Native population

© HMH Supplemental Publishers Inc.

NAME _____

CAPITALIZE THE FIRST WORD OF A SENTENCE

 Every sentence begins with a capital letter. Make sure you capitalize the first word of a sentence.

Our class is learning about early settlers.

Early settlers in Texas lived by the Red River.

Write each sentence correctly.

1. today our class visited Pioneer Farm.

_____

2. what is Pioneer Farm?

_____

3. it is a living museum.

_____

4. we saw log cabins and barns.

_____

5. did people dress in old-fashioned clothes?

_____

6. yes, and they showed quilting and blacksmithing.

_____

© HMH Supplemental Publishers Inc.

NAME

EDITING FOR GRAMMAR, SPELLING, AND PUNCTUATION

See also pages 180 and 181.

 A verb must agree with its subject.

I am here.   *She is here.*   *We are here.*

 The present progressive tense of a verb shows a continuing action. It uses *am, is,* or *are* and a verb that ends in *–ing*.

I am eating lunch.   *They are going away.*

The future tense of a verb shows action that will happen in the future. It uses the helping verb *will* plus the main verb.

Tomorrow we will visit my aunt.

Listen to your teacher. Compare the first draft of the practice paragraph to the edited draft.

The flu are a disease. Sneezing and coughing can spread the germs that cause the flu. Doctors are study the problem. They gives these tips. Cover your mouth when you sneeze or cough so germs do not spread. When you touch things that have flu germs on them, the germs gets on your hands. they get in your body when you rub your eyes or touch parts of your face. So, wash your hands often. If you follow these tips, you will helped prevent flu germs from spreading.

The flu is a disease. Sneezing and coughing can spread the germs that cause the flu. Doctors are studying the problem. They give these tips. Cover your mouth when you sneeze or cough so germs do not spread. When you touch things that have flu germs on them, the germs get on your hands. They get in your body when you rub your eyes or touch parts of your face. So, wash your hands often. If you follow these tips, you will help prevent flu germs from spreading.

© HMH Supplemental Publishers Inc.

NAME _____

READER'S LOG: "JOURNEY ON THE ROYAL ROAD"

BEFORE READING: PAIR AND SHARE

1. My class talked about the _____.

   ☐ title   ☐ illustrations   ☐ _____

2. I understood _____ of the discussion.

   ☐ most or all   ☐ some   ☐ little or none

DURING READING

3. What are the major events in the story?

   _____

   _____

   _____

   _____

4. Is there anything in the story that you do not understand? Write about it here:

   _____

   _____

   _____

AFTER READING: PAIR AND SHARE

5. Talk to your partner about anything that you did not understand.

Now, my partner and I understand _____.

Me   ☐ a lot better   ☐ a little better   ☐ no better

My partner ☐ a lot better   ☐ a little better   ☐ no better

© HMH Supplemental Publishers Inc.

NAME _____

WHICH WORD AM I?

Read the clues. Write the correct vocabulary word from the box to match each clue.

expedition	hardship	frontier	wagon	caravan	pioneer

1. I am a group of people who travel together for safety on a challenging trip.

_____

2. I am a long trip that has a purpose.

_____

3. I am one of the first people to settle a place.

_____

4. I am a vehicle with four wheels, pulled by horses.

_____

5. I am the open land beyond all settled areas.

_____

6. I am something that causes problems or challenges.

_____

© HMH Supplemental Publishers Inc.

NAME _____

UNSCRAMBLE THE WORDS

Unscramble each word to spell one of the words in the box. Write the word on the line under the scrambled word.

HISTORIC	GOVERN	DEPEND	GUIDE
	MISSION	STEAMBOAT	

1. SIMNISO (a church)

_____

2. ATTEBOMAS (a boat that is powered by steam engines)

_____

3. CHITSROI (important to our history)

_____

4. EGIDU (a person who shows people a new place and gives them information about the place)

_____

5. RONVGE (to rule over a place and help make laws for the people who live there)

_____

6. EDDNEP (to rely on or need)

_____

© HMH Supplemental Publishers Inc.

NAME ————————————————————————

A. Asking Questions

Look at the picture. Which question best fits the picture?

1. What is the best question?

   A Who are you?

   B What is the girl saying?

   C How much is it?

2. What is the best question?

   A Where is he going?

   B What is Mom doing?

   C Do you like cars?

B. Choosing the Verb Tense

Read the sentence. Which verb tense is used?

3. The girl is kicking the ball.

   A present tense

   B future tense

   C past tense

4. Yesterday, my brother helped me.

   A present tense

   B future tense

   C past tense

© HMH Supplemental Publishers Inc.

NAME _____

C. Present or Present Progressive Tense

Look at the picture. Read the sentences. Circle the letter of the BEST sentence to describe the picture.

5.

A They are talking about their plans.

B They sometimes write stories.

6. Tell why you think the sentence you chose is best.

_____

_____

_____

_____

_____

PAIR AND SHARE Discuss what you do every day and what you are doing right now. Use these sentence frames:

A. Ask questions.

1. *What do you do most every day?*

2. *What are you doing right now?*

B. Answer the questions.

1. *Every day, I _____.* (eat breakfast, read books, study math, talk to friends)

2. *Right now, I am _____.* (talking to you, doing my homework, sitting in class)

Check page 180 to review the simple present tense and the present progressive action verbs.

Monitor Language: How's your grammar?

Listen to your partner. Were the present and present progressive verb forms correct?

Yes, always	Sometimes	Never
☐	☐	☐

How were your verb tenses and forms? Were they correct?

Yes, always	Sometimes	Never
☐	☐	☐

© HMH Supplemental Publishers Inc.

NAME —————————————————————————————————

CLOSE READING OF THE TEXT

 Self-monitor your understanding as you read.

1. **Reread.** Start with the last sentence you understood. Then read on from that point.

2. **Take notes.** Write down the most important details. This can help you understand and remember what you read.

3. **Look up words you don't know.**

4. **Ask questions.** Then look for answers to your questions in the text, or you can ask someone.

Interview Text	Notes
Carlota: *What is the Alamo?* **Guide:** The Alamo is a mission. The Spanish built it in the 1700s. Priests lived here. Back then, Texas was part of Mexico, and Mexico was ruled by Spain. In 1821, Mexico—and Texas—won their independence from Spain.	Underline anything you do not understand. Take notes. What are the most important ideas? _____ _____ _____
Carlota: *Did anything important happen here?* **Guide:** Yes. The Alamo is where Tejanos and Texans fought a battle against Mexico.	Tell what you reread or a question you asked. _____ _____ _____ _____

© HMH Supplemental Publishers Inc.

95

NAME _____

READ WITH EXPRESSION

Read the following section of poetry aloud. Read with energy and strong emotion. Pause for punctuation marks such as commas and periods. Listen to your partner's reading. Then practice the passage a second time.

Note: One slash (/) indicates a short pause for a comma. Two slashes (//) indicates a longer pause for a period.

John Henry said to his boss, /

"I am just a man, /

But before I let your drill beat me down, /

I'll die with my hammer in my hand." //

John Henry held his hammer. //

Beside the steam drill he did stand. //

He beat that steam drill three inches down

And died with his hammer in his hand. //

And every time that train goes by, /

They say, / "There lies a hard working man. //

There lies a hard working man." //

© HMH Supplemental Publishers Inc.

NAME —————————————————————————————

CHECK YOUR UNDERSTANDING

A. Reread "Journey on the Royal Road," on **Student Edition** pages 212–217. Then read each sentence below. Circle the letter of the correct answer.

1. The Sosaya family pack their _____ with food and their belongings.

A wagon

C possessions

B chicken coops

D pioneer

2. The Sosayas start their trip during the _____.

A spring

C fall

B summer

D winter

© HMH Supplemental Publishers Inc.

NAME _____

B. Read each sentence below. Circle the letter of the correct answer.

3. Catalina worries that _____.

   A thieves will attack their caravan

   B her family will never reach California

   C they will soon join other pioneer families

   D they will not find a place to make camp

4. One hardship that the Sosayas face is _____.

   A being robbed by thieves

   B getting stuck in a dust storm

   C stopping to make camp

   D collecting eggs from the chickens

C. Read each question below. Circle the letter of the correct answer.

5. What might people who traveled to California on El Camino Real be excited about?

   A the dangers of the journey

   B hiding valuable possessions from thieves

   C starting a new life in a new place

   D getting stuck in dust storms

6. During which month might the Sosayas have arrived in California?

   A January

   B April

   C August

   D November

© HMH Supplemental Publishers Inc.

NAME _____

A. Label

Write a word that names each picture. Use a word from the word box.

| bread | bed | con | hockey | hook | coin | box | toll |

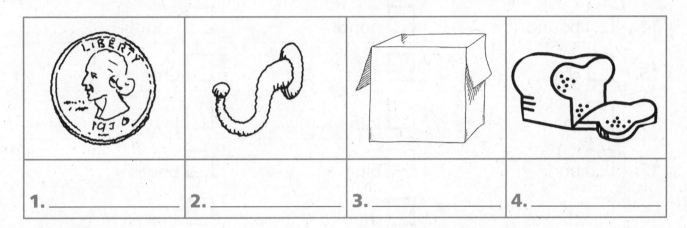

1. _____ 2. _____ 3. _____ 4. _____

B. Phonics

Read these words aloud. Use the phonics skills you have learned.

	A	B	C	D	E	F	G
5.	toy	stew	found	tea	book	moon	notebook
6.	soy	blue	house	sea	cook	troop	excite
7.	boy	chew	mouse	pea	rook	room	female
8.	coin	glue	loud	seat	took	cool	tadpole
9.	soil	few	out	bead	hook	proof	escape
10.	coil	true	about	treat	look	hoop	unmade

C. High-Frequency Words

Read these words aloud.

11.	their	if	will	up	other	about
12.	out	many	them	all	these	some

© HMH Supplemental Publishers Inc.

NAME _____

D. Listen. Read. Check.

Your teacher will say a word. Mark the box next to the word.

13.	☐ few	☐ food	☐ foot
14.	☐ pound	☐ pond	☐ pun
15.	☐ cheat	☐ chat	☐ Chet
16.	☐ Joan	☐ join	☐ joy
17.	☐ boo	☐ blue	☐ boot
18.	☐ choke	☐ shook	☐ shake
19.	☐ sun	☐ soon	☐ sound
20.	☐ joke	☐ go	☐ Joe

E. Spelling

Your teacher will say a word. Write the word. Check your spelling.

21. _____   23. _____

22. _____   24. _____

© HMH Supplemental Publishers Inc.

NAME

CHECKLIST

Word	I've never heard of it.	I've heard of it.	I know what it means.
communicate	☐	☐	☐
technology	☐	☐	☐
innovation	☐	☐	☐
satellite	☐	☐	☐
telegraph	☐	☐	☐
invention	☐	☐	☐
device	☐	☐	☐
model	☐	☐	☐

Which word did you find most challenging?

_____

© HMH Supplemental Publishers Inc.

NAME _____

CHECKLIST

Word	I've never heard of it.	I've heard of it.	I know what it means.
impact	☐	☐	☐
patent	☐	☐	☐
labor	☐	☐	☐
online	☐	☐	☐
improve	☐	☐	☐
medicine	☐	☐	☐
explosion	☐	☐	☐
develop	☐	☐	☐

Which word did you find most interesting?

_____

© HMH Supplemental Publishers Inc.

NAME _____

READING LONGER WORDS

Reading Vowel Pair Syllables

Two vowel letters often stand for one sound. Example: *keep*

You can divide:
- between the words in a compound word.
- after a prefix, or before a suffix.
- between the consonants in a VCCV letter pattern.
- before or after the consonant in a VCV letter pattern.

A. Divide the word. Circle the vowel pair. Read each syllable.
Then read the whole word.

n e e d e d	l o u d l y	w e e k l y
w o o d e n	b r a i d e d	s l e e p i n g

B. Divide the word. Circle the vowel pair. Read each syllable.
Then read the whole word.

n o t e b o o k	p e a n u t	c l a s s r o o m	h a n d r a i l
r o w b o a t	t e x t b o o k	c u t o u t	b o w t i e

C. Divide the word. Read each syllable. Then read the whole word.

b e l o w	m e a d o w	e m u

D. Divide the word. Read each syllable. Then read the whole word.

e l b o w	m u s h r o o m	s h a m p o o	e x p l a i n
r o w b o a t	w i n d o w	r a i n b o w	i g l o o

© HMH Supplemental Publishers Inc.

NAME _____

RUBRIC: PROCEDURAL TEXT

When you write a procedural text, check it against this rubric.
Did you do everything you can to make it better?　Yes ☐　No ☐

Cell Phone Rescue	Charles's Model	Class Model	My Model
1. A title describes the project or activity.			
2. There is a list of necessary materials or tools.			
3. Photos or illustrations may show the steps or final product.			
4. Numbered steps tell how to do a task.			
5. Each step is written clearly.			
6. Words and numbers make the order of the steps clear.			
7. The document is neat and easy to read.			
8. The grammar, spelling, and punctuation are correct.			

Score

3. Excellent　　2. Good　　1. Needs work

© HMH Supplemental Publishers Inc.

NAME

ORGANIZER: PROCEDURAL TEXT

Materials needed:

First,

Second,

Third,

Next,

Finally. . .

© HMH Supplemental Publishers Inc.

NAME _____

USING COMMAS IN SENTENCES

> **i** Commas tell a reader where to pause.
>
> Use commas to separate three or more items in a series.
> *Computers, cell phones, and calculators make life easier.*
>
> Use a comma to separate the parts of a compound sentence.
> *Cell phones make keeping in touch easier, and calculators make math easier.*
>
> Use a comma after the words *yes* and *no* when they begin a sentence.
> *Yes, I love computers!*
>
> Use a comma to set off the name of a person you are speaking to.
> *Marie, please print me a copy of your report.*

Write each sentence correctly. Use commas where needed.

1. Cell phones can make calls take photos and play music.

_____

_____

2. Rita would you please turn on the computer?

_____

3. Eduardo will play and Beatriz will sing.

_____

4. I will research coal and wood.

_____

5. No we can't stop now.

_____

© HMH Supplemental Publishers Inc.

© HMH Supplemental Publishers Inc.

NAME _____

EDITING FOR GRAMMAR, SPELLING, AND PUNCTUATION

See also page 175.

 The verb *make* is regular in the present tense. The verbs *go, do,* and *have* are irregular.

I, we, you, they	make	go	do	have
he, she, it	makes	**goes**	**does**	**has**

 The verbs *go, do, have,* and *make* are irregular in the past tense.

Verb	go	do	have	make
Past Tense	went	did	had	made

 Form the possessive of most singular nouns by adding *'s*.
the dog's bone   my sister's car

Listen to your teacher. Compare the first draft of the practice paragraph to the edited draft.

Every summer, my family ⟨gos⟩ to the beach. We stay at my uncles house. Last summer, my leg was in a cast. Did I want to go to the beach? No, I ⟨does⟩ not! I ⟨maked⟩ up my mind that I would be bored sad and miserable. My mom solved the problem. She ⟨haved⟩ a plastic bag that fit over my cast. I couldn't swim but I could enjoy the beach.

Every summer, my family goes to the beach. We stay at my uncle's house. Last summer, my leg was in a cast. Did I want to go to the beach? No, I did not! I made up my mind that I would be bored, sad, and miserable. My mom solved the problem. She had a plastic bag that fit over my cast. I couldn't swim, but I could enjoy the beach.

NAME _____

READER'S LOG: "MARGARET KNIGHT: A LIFETIME OF INVENTIONS!"

BEFORE READING: PAIR AND SHARE

1. My class talked about the _____.

   ☐ title   ☐ illustrations   ☐ _____

2. I understood _____ of the discussion.

   ☐ most or all   ☐ some   ☐ little or none

DURING READING

3. What kind of person do you think Margaret Knight was? Why do you think so?

   _____

   _____

4. Is there anything in the selection that you do not understand? Write about it here:

   _____

AFTER READING: PAIR AND SHARE

5. Talk to your partner about anything in the story that you do not understand.

   Now, my partner and I understand _____.

   Me   ☐ a lot better   ☐ a little better   ☐ no better

   My partner   ☐ a lot better   ☐ a little better   ☐ no better

© HMH Supplemental Publishers Inc.

NAME _____

MATCH IT UP

Write the letter of the definition that matches each word.

1. _____ satellite

A a tool that is made to do a special job

2. _____ device

B something that someone has made for the first time

3. _____ communicate

C a machine that sends electrical messages over wire

4. _____ telegraph

D share your ideas, thoughts, or feelings with someone else

5. _____ model

E a small copy of something

6. _____ invention

F a manufactured object that is sent into space to move around Earth

© HMH Supplemental Publishers Inc.

NAME

SYNONYMS

Read each sentence. Write the vocabulary word from the box that has the same meaning as the word or words in bold print.

| labor | medicine | impact | develop | online | improve |

1. We can add new wheels to our cart to **make it better**.

_____

2. You can look for news articles **on the Internet** or in a printed magazine.

_____

3. The music had a strong **effect** on Raúl's life and made him want to become a musician.

_____

4. It took months of long, hard **work** to build the railroad.

_____

5. Talia wants to **make** a new kind of bicycle.

_____

6. My aunt wants to study the **treatment of diseases**.

_____

© HMH Supplemental Publishers Inc.

NAME

A. Subject and Object Pronouns

Look at the picture. Read the sentence. Which word can replace the underlined words?

1. Anna kicks <u>the ball</u>!

   A she   **C** it

   B her   **D** them

2. <u>My parents</u> make the dinner.

   A Them   **C** It

   B They   **D** He

B. Combining Sentences

Which sentence **best** combines the information in the first two sentences?

3. Mr. Kim has a lot of books.
   I like his books.

   A I like Mr. Kim's books.

   B They are Mr. Kims books.

   C I like books.

4. The baby has toys.
   They are broken.

   A The babys toys are broken.

   B The baby's toys are broken.

   C Break the baby's toys.

© HMH Supplemental Publishers Inc.

NAME _____

C. Irregular Past-Tense Verbs

Choose the verb that best fits the sentence.

5. They sing very loud. Last week, they _____ in a concert.

   A sing   **C** is singing

   B sang   **D** will sing

6. My brother makes popcorn. Last week, he _____ a big mess!

   A make   **C** will make

   B makes   **D** made

PAIR AND SHARE With your partner, discuss what each of you or one other person owns.

Use these sentence frames:

A. Ask a question.

   Whose _____ *is that?* (book, pencil, pen, car)

B. Answer the question.

   That is _____. (Miguel's book, the teacher's desk, my mother's jacket)

Check page 177 to review how to say that someone owns something. Be sure to pronounce the 's.

Monitor Language: How's your grammar?

Listen to your partner. Was the correct possessive form used? Was the 's pronounced?

Yes, always	Sometimes	Never
☐	☐	☐

How were your possessive forms? Were they correct? Did you pronounce 's?

Yes, always	Sometimes	Never
☐	☐	☐

© HMH Supplemental Publishers Inc.

NAME —

CLOSE READING OF THE TEXT

 Self-monitor your understanding as you read.

1. **Reread**. Start with the last sentences you understood. Then read on from that point.

2. **Take notes**. Write down the most important details. This can help you understand and remember what you read.

3. **Look up words you don't know.**

4. **Ask questions**. Then look for answers to your questions in the text, or you can ask someone.

Historical Fiction	Notes
Jun Ming had left his home in China to work for the Central Pacific Railroad Company. Many of his friends and family followed. Now they worked for the company, too. They were helping to build the first transcontinental railroad across the United States. Each day of labor was long and hard. Jun Ming got up before sunrise, and he worked on the railroad until long after dark. He dug holes, cleared rocks, shoveled dirt, and built bridges. He laid the railroad ties and iron rails. Every night his back and arms ached, and his legs were sore.	Underline anything you do not understand. Take notes. What are the most important ideas? _____ _____ _____ Tell what you reread or a question you asked. _____ _____ _____

© HMH Supplemental Publishers Inc.

NAME _____

READ FOR ACCURACY

Work with a partner. Take turns reading the passage aloud. Try to speak clearly and pronounce each word correctly. Then review the passage together. Write the difficult words on the lines below. Practice saying the words aloud. Then read the passage a second time.

> ### From "Playing It Safe on the Web"
>
> First, never talk to strangers on the Web. You should communicate only with people you know and trust.
>
> Second, remember that if anyone online talks about something or uses language that makes you uncomfortable, don't respond! Log off and tell an adult.
>
> Third, never give your last name, address, telephone number, or password to anyone. A person you meet online may be pretending to be someone else.

© HMH Supplemental Publishers Inc.

_____ _____

_____ _____

_____ _____

_____ _____

NAME ——————————————————————————————————————

CHECK YOUR UNDERSTANDING

A. Reread "Margaret Knight: A Lifetime of Inventions!" on **Student Edition** pages 258–267. Then read each sentence below. Circle the letter of the correct answer.

1. Margaret's invention stopped workers from getting _____ .

   A hurt   **C** fired

   B lost   **D** weak

2. After the court case, _____ got the patent for the machine to make paper bags.

   A the judge   **C** Margaret

   B the lawyer   **D** the man

© HMH Supplemental Publishers Inc.

NAME _____

B. Read each sentence below. Circle the letter of the correct answer.

3. When Margaret Knight was a girl, she _____.

   A built a machine to make paper bags

   B invented toys for her brothers

   C went to court to get a patent

   D had no interest in inventions

4. Margaret made drawings, and next she made _____ of her machine.

   A a wooden model

   B an iron model

   C a copy

   D a design on paper

C. Read each question below. Circle the letter of the correct answer.

5. Why did Margaret show the judge her notes, drawings, and models?

   A to show that the paper bag machine would work

   B to share her ideas about paper bags with the judge

   C to show she was a better inventor than the man

   D to prove she had been working on the machine for a long time

6. Why was the paper bag such an important invention?

   A It meant Margaret was a real inventor.

   B It meant businesses could help shoppers faster.

   C It meant workers were safer and would not get hurt.

   D It encouraged other women to become inventors.

© HMH Supplemental Publishers Inc.

NAME

A. Label

Write a word that names the picture. Use a word from the word box.

crow	cow	car	star	hook	foot	fur	core

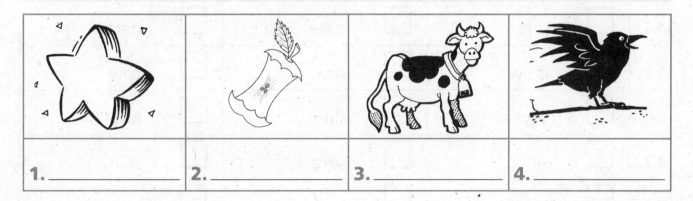

1. _____
2. _____
3. _____
4. _____

B. Phonics

Read the words aloud. Use the phonics skills you have learned.

	A	B	C	D	E	F	G
5.	crow	cow	car	soar	bird	burn	railroad
6.	show	now	tar	more	fern	fur	dugout
7.	blow	wow	start	porch	word	herd	proceed
8.	grow	town	part	score	fur	stir	release
9.	low	owl	chart	for	sir	purr	repeat
10.	slow	how	lark	poor	turn	her	midweek

C. High-Frequency Words

Read the words aloud.

11.	her	would	make	like	him	into
12.	time	has	look	two	more	write

© HMH Supplemental Publishers Inc.

NAME _____

D. Listen. Read. Check.

Your teacher will say a word. Mark the box next to the word.

13.	☐ mark		☐ make		☐ mock
14.	☐ dirt		☐ date		☐ dart
15.	☐ crow		☐ row		☐ cow
16.	☐ sow		☐ slow		☐ low
17.	☐ sir		☐ sore		☐ shark
18.	☐ herd		☐ her		☐ hurt
19.	☐ park		☐ part		☐ par
20.	☐ sheer		☐ sharp		☐ chart

E. Spelling

Your teacher will say a word. Write the word. Check your spelling.

21. _____   23. _____

22. _____   24. _____

© HMH Supplemental Publishers Inc.

© HMH Supplemental Publishers Inc.

NAME ——————————————————

MONITORING LISTENING CHECKLIST

	Unit 7	Unit 8	End of Book
	Earth, Moon, and Sun	**Pulse of Life**	
1. What is the topic?			
2. The general meaning of the discussion was ___.			
3. The words and sentences were mostly ___.	☐ clear ☐ confusing	☐ clear ☐ confusing	☐ clear ☐ confusing
4. Some of the important details include ___.			
5. I ask for help when I don't understand.	☐ usually ☐ sometimes ☐ never	☐ usually ☐ sometimes ☐ never	☐ usually ☐ sometimes ☐ never
6. The way I understand discussions has ___.	☐ improved ☐ stayed the same	☐ improved ☐ stayed the same	☐ improved ☐ stayed the same

NAME _____

CHECKLIST

Word	I've never heard of it.	I've heard of it.	I know what it means.
distance	☐	☐	☐
inner planets	☐	☐	☐
outer planets	☐	☐	☐
astronomy	☐	☐	☐
axis	☐	☐	☐
rover	☐	☐	☐
revolve	☐	☐	☐
oxygen	☐	☐	☐

Which word did you find most challenging?

_____

© HMH Supplemental Publishers Inc.

NAME _____

CHECKLIST

Word	I've never heard of it.	I've heard of it.	I know what it means.
crater	☐	☐	☐
spacecraft	☐	☐	☐
equipment	☐	☐	☐
flight	☐	☐	☐
space station	☐	☐	☐
launch	☐	☐	☐
lunar	☐	☐	☐
telescope	☐	☐	☐

Which word did you find most interesting?

_____

© HMH Supplemental Publishers Inc.

NAME _____

MONITORING SPEAKING CHECKLIST

	Unit 7	Unit 8	End of Book
	"King of the Game"	"A Big Pain"	
1. I can retell the story by describing the ___.	☐ beginning ☐ middle ☐ end	☐ beginning ☐ middle ☐ end	☐ beginning ☐ middle ☐ end
2. I can support my opinions, ideas, and feelings about the story ___.	☐ all of the time ☐ often ☐ sometimes	☐ all of the time ☐ often ☐ sometimes	☐ all of the time ☐ often ☐ sometimes
3. I can describe and explain what I want to say ___.	☐ all of the time ☐ often ☐ sometimes	☐ all of the time ☐ often ☐ sometimes	☐ all of the time ☐ often ☐ sometimes
4. The way I can make myself understood has ___.	☐ improved ☐ stayed the same ☐ gotten worse	☐ improved ☐ stayed the same ☐ gotten worse	☐ improved ☐ stayed the same ☐ gotten worse
5. How do you explain your answer to #4, above?			

© HMH Supplemental Publishers Inc.

NAME _____

READING LONGER WORDS

 Reading Syllables with Vowel + *r*

When a vowel is followed by letter *r*, the sound of the vowel sometimes changes.

Examples: *her, bird, girl, pearl, cart, cork*

 You can divide:

between the words in a compound word.

after a prefix, or before a suffix.

between the consonants in a VCCV letter pattern.

before or after the consonant in a VCV letter pattern.

Divide the word. Read each syllable. Then read the whole word.

started	curling	artist	taller	worker

Divide the word. Read each syllable. Then read the whole word.

birthday	bluebird	homework
offshore	pitchfork	boxcar

Divide the word. Read each syllable. Then read the whole word.

diner	baker	tiger
liver	ever	cower

Divide the word. Read each syllable. Then read the whole word.
Remember: Digraphs such as *ch*, *th*, **and** *sh* **act as one letter.**

concert	turnip	further	burger

© HMH Supplemental Publishers Inc.

NAME _____

NARRATIVE RUBRIC: Science Fiction

When you write a science fiction narrative, check it against this rubric.
Did you do all you can to make it better?   Yes ☐   No ☐

	Awesome Planet	Jill's Model	Class Model	My Model
1.	Science fiction is a type of narrative that comes from the writer's imagination, but is located in such settings as the *future* or *space*.			
2.	It is clear **where** and **when** the story takes place.			
3.	It is told in the third person using proper nouns *he, she,* or *they.*			
4.	The story reveals the characters through what they say and do.			
5.	The actions follow each other in a logical way.			
6.	Words help explain the order.			
7.	It may use realistic dialogue to make the characters come alive.			
8.	The ending seems right for the story.			
9.	Readers will like the story!			

Score
3: Excellent   2: Good   1. Needs work

© HMH Supplemental Publishers Inc.

NAME

NARRATIVE SEQUENCE ORGANIZER

1. Captain Xing enters spaceship's Situation Room.

2. He worries that they won't find a new planet to call home.

3. An image of another planet appears.

4. Conditions on this planet look extremely favorable.

5. This new planet is called *Earth.*

© HMH Supplemental Publishers Inc.

NAME _____

USING QUOTATION MARKS FOR SPEECH

> ⓘ Use quotation marks to show a speaker's exact words.
>
> Quotation marks go before and after a speaker's words.
> *"I like movies," said Ned.*
>
> Punctuation for a speaker's words goes inside the quotation marks.
> *"That's the best movie I've ever seen!" Anna said.*
>
> A comma separates a speaker's words from the rest of the sentence.
> *Ned said, "Meet me outside the theater."*
>
> A comma takes the place of a period inside quotation marks if it isn't the end of the whole sentence.
> *"I'll be there," Anna replied.*

Write each sentence correctly. Use quotation marks where needed.

1. My dad said Let's go to the movies.

_____

2. What will we see? I asked.

_____

3. First, let's find out what's playing Dad replied.

_____

4. I asked, Are there any funny movies?

_____

5. Dad answered I hope so!

_____

© HMH Supplemental Publishers Inc.

NAME _____

EDITING FOR GRAMMAR, SPELLING, AND PUNCTUATION

See also pages 177, 178, and 182.

> To show possession of a plural noun ending in *–s* or *–es*, add an apostrophe to the end of the word.
> *the actors' lines*   *the houses' addresses*

> To show possession of a plural noun that does not end in *–s* or *–es*, add *'s* to the end of the word.
> *the children's performance*   *the men's choir*

> In English, use only one negative word in a sentence. Some examples of negative words are *never, no, nobody, none, not, nothing,* and *nowhere.* Using two of these words in the same sentence is incorrect and is called a "double negative."
> Incorrect: *They could not see nothing in the dark.*
> Correct: *They could see nothing in the dark.*
> Correct: *They could not see anything in the dark.*

Listen to your teacher. Compare the first draft of the practice paragraph to the edited draft.

Tim asked Did you see the show about dogs last night? I told him that I don't never watch TV. Tim's eyes showed surprise. "It was great! he said. "It showed amazing dogs. They found people buried under snow. They pulled people out of fires. Some dogs's bravery is incredible! I couldn't never do what those dogs did. You must watch the show with me if it plays again."

Tim asked, "Did you see the show about dogs last night?" I told him that I never watch TV. Tim's eyes showed surprise. "It was great!" he said. "It showed amazing dogs. They found people buried under snow. They pulled people out of fires. Some dogs' bravery is incredible! I could never do what those dogs did. You must watch the show with me if it plays again."

© HMH Supplemental Publishers Inc.

NAME _____

READER'S LOG: "MOON GAMES"

> ℹ️ Active listeners take notes. Active readers do, too. Write only
> the most important information.

PAIR AND SHARE Reread the selection with your partner. Mark the boxes
and take notes as you read. Add to your notes as you talk to your partner.

1. How difficult is the selection?

☐ very difficult   ☐ not too difficult   ☐ easy

2. What makes the selection difficult?

☐ the words   ☐ the information   ☐ everything!

3. List the most difficult words.

_____

4. What did you do about the difficult words?

☐ We talked about them.   ☐ We looked at the pictures.

☐ We looked them up in a dictionary.   ☐ We asked our teacher.

5. What did you learn from the pictures?

_____

6. Are there any sentences that you don't understand?

Note the page number, and ask your teacher what they mean. _____

© HMH Supplemental Publishers Inc.

NAME _____

USE CLUES

Read each sentence. Use context clues to help you figure out the correct vocabulary word from the box to complete each sentence. Write the word on the line.

revolves	distance	inner planets	oxygen
	astronomy	rover	

1. When we breathe, our bodies use _____ from the air.

_____

2. Our class studied the _____, which are the four planets closest to the sun.

_____

3. Earth _____ around the sun once every 365 days.

_____

4. The sign says that the _____ to Austin is fifty-five miles.

_____

5. Scientists sent a _____ to Mars to gather information so they could learn more about the planet.

_____

6. People study _____ to learn about the sun and the planets.

_____

© HMH Supplemental Publishers Inc.

NAME _____

WHICH WORD AM I?

Read the clues. Write the correct vocabulary word from the box to match each clue.

spacecraft	space station	telescope
crater	flight	equipment

1. I am a tool you can use to look at objects that are very far away.

_____

2. I am a trip in the air or in space.

_____

3. I am a structure in space where people live and work.

_____

4. I am the things needed or used for a certain purpose.

_____

5. I am a bowl-shaped hole made when something very big hits the ground.

_____

6. I am a vehicle that is used to travel in space.

_____

© HMH Supplemental Publishers Inc.

NAME ———————————————————————————————

A. Using Negatives

Look at the picture. Read the question. Circle the correct answer.

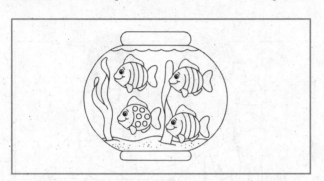

1. Are five goldfish in the bowl?

   A Yes, five goldfish are in the bowl.

   B No, five goldfish aren't in the bowl.

   C Yes, I see goldfish.

2. Is Lin in the house?

   A No, she isn't in the house.

   B Lin likes kites.

   C Lin doesn't see nothing.

B. Plural Possessive Nouns

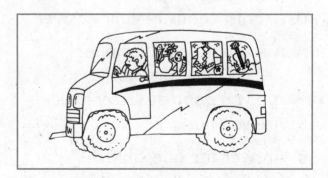

3. My two cousins own a cat. Is she cute?

   A No, my cat isn't cute.

   B Yes, my cousin's cat is cute.

   C Yes, my cousins' cat is cute.

4. Does this van belong to both of your parents?

   A No, it isn't my parents' van.

   B No, it isn't my parent's van.

   C Yes, I see my parents.

© HMH Supplemental Publishers Inc.

NAME _____

C. Combining Sentences

Read the two sentences. Which sentence best combines the meaning of the two sentences?

5. The dog runs. The cats just sit.

   A John has a cat and dog.

   B The dog runs, but the cats just sit.

   C Dogs can't sit.

6. The book belongs to Sari. It belongs to her sister, too.

   A The book is theirs.

   B They are sitting there.

   C They can read.

PAIR AND SHARE Ask questions that can be answered *yes* or *no*. Use contractions in your answer.

A. Ask questions. Examples:
   Are you 15 years old?
   Are you good at soccer?
   Are you hungry?

B. Answer the questions.
   No, I'm not 15 years old.
   Yes, I'm good at soccer.
   No, I'm not hungry.

Check pages 171–172 to review using contractions.

Monitor Language: How's your grammar?

Listen to your partner. Was the question answered? Was a contraction used correctly?

Yes, always	Sometimes	Never
☐	☐	☐

Did you answer the question and correctly use contractions?

Yes, always	Sometimes	Never
☐	☐	☐

© HMH Supplemental Publishers Inc.

NAME —————————————————————————————

CLOSE READING OF THE TEXT

 Self-monitor your understanding as you read.

1. **Reread.** Start with the last sentences you understood. Then read on from that point.

2. **Take notes.** Write down the most important details. This can help you understand and remember what you read.

3. **Look up words you don't know.**

4. **Ask questions.** Then look for answers to your questions in the text, or you can ask someone.

Informative Text	Notes
Eating Everything in space floats weightlessly, so astronauts must strap their trays of food to their thighs. Magnets keep their forks on their trays. Drinks are put in special packets so they don't flow out. **Sleeping** If astronauts tried to sleep in beds like yours, they would float right out. In space, they have to stay in sleeping bags strapped to the wall. The cabins that they use for bedrooms are only as big as shower stalls.	Underline anything you do not understand. Take notes. What are the most important ideas? _____ _____ _____ Tell what you reread or a question you asked. _____ _____ _____

© HMH Supplemental Publishers Inc.

NAME _____

READ FOR RATE

Read the following passage aloud. Have a partner time your reading for one minute. Then, fill in the chart at the bottom of the page with the number of words you read. Read the passage a second and third time. Try to increase the number of words you read accurately in a minute.

This spring, two skillful astronauts took a space walk to	10
improve safety on the International Space Station. The	18
astronauts were Astronaut Franklin Chang-Díaz, a Costa Rican-	27
born American, and his French crewmate, Phillippe Pérrin.	35
They hung upside down outside the space station. Then they	45
carefully attached metal shields to make the space station	54
safer.	55
The shields protect the living area from harmful objects that	65
sometimes crash into the space station. This equipment is	74
important to the safety of the astronauts. Chang-Díaz said he	85
felt quite strange floating above Earth. However, Pérrin	93
seemed to enjoy hanging upside down like a bat.	102

Number of Words Read		
First Reading	Second Reading	Third Reading

© HMH Supplemental Publishers Inc.

NAME ————————————————————————————

CHECK YOUR UNDERSTANDING

A. Reread "Moon Games" on **Student Edition** pages 304–313. Then read each sentence below. Circle the letter of the correct answer.

1. Felipe is going to compete on _____ .

   A Earth   **C** Jupiter

   B Saturn   **D** the Moon

2. Saturn has _____ .

   A rings around it   **C** a continent that looks like North America

   B 60 moons   **D** an athletic competition that Felipe is going to

© HMH Supplemental Publishers Inc.

NAME _____

B. Read each sentence below. Circle the letter of the correct answer.

3. This selection is _____.

    A realistic fiction

    B a play that happens in an imagined future

    C a story written by a boy from the future

    D an article about gravity and the planets

4. Felipe gets to travel to the Moon because _____.

    A his great-grandmother was a space traveler and inventor

    B he won an athletic competition in Washington, DC

    C his whole class is going there

    D he is part of his school athletic team

C. Read each question below. Circle the letter of the correct answer.

5. Why does Felipe train at an "anti-gravity stadium"?

    A It is easier to lift weights without gravity.

    B There is no gravity during the flight to the Moon.

    C There is very little gravity on the Moon.

    D That's the best way to get strong

6. Which of the following is NOT a made-up idea about the future?

    A In 2064 people will eat food from tubes.

    B In the future, people from all different planets will compete together.

    C People in 2064 will be able to travel 50,000 miles an hour.

    D The surface of the Moon is sandy and rocky, and covered with craters.

© HMH Supplemental Publishers Inc.

NAME

A. Label

Write a word that names the picture. Use a word from the word box.

| chill | child | foal | fold | rid | car | fur | words |

1. _____

2. _____

3. _____

4. _____

B. Phonics

Read the words aloud. Use the phonics skills you have learned.

	A	B	C	D	E	F	G
5.	bore	fir	bind	sold	law	after	perfect
6.	soar	pure	kind	bold	saw	artist	thirsty
7.	core	word	find	cold	taught	dirty	garlic
8.	for	her	wild	hold	caught	disturb	fairway
9.	shore	shirt	child	fold	raw	forty	favor
10.	or	cure	mild	gold	paw	pattern	summer

C. High-Frequency Words

Read the words aloud.

| 11. | see | number | way | could | people | my |
| 12. | than | first | water | been | call | who |

© HMH Supplemental Publishers Inc.

NAME _____

D. Listen. Read. Check.

Your teacher will say a word. Mark the box next to the word.

13.	☐ mode	☐ mole	☐ mold
14.	☐ mine	☐ mind	☐ mint
15.	☐ rare	☐ roar	☐ row
16.	☐ pure	☐ peer	☐ pair
17.	☐ roll	☐ ram	☐ raw
18.	☐ tall	☐ talk	☐ told
19.	☐ bur	☐ bird	☐ bear
20.	☐ wild	☐ will	☐ wail

E. Spelling

Your teacher will say a word. Write the word. Check your spelling.

21. _____   23. _____

22. _____   24. _____

© HMH Supplemental Publishers Inc.

NAME —————————————————————————

CHECKLIST

Word	I've never heard of it.	I've heard of it.	I know what it means.
coordinate	☐	☐	☐
emotion	☐	☐	☐
voluntary	☐	☐	☐
involuntary	☐	☐	☐
respiration	☐	☐	☐
photosynthesis	☐	☐	☐
chlorophyll	☐	☐	☐
nutrients	☐	☐	☐

Which word did you find most challenging?

—————————————————————————————————

© HMH Supplemental Publishers Inc.

NAME _____

CHECKLIST

Word	I've never heard of it.	I've heard of it.	I know what it means.
characteristic	☐	☐	☐
network	☐	☐	☐
nerves	☐	☐	☐
pulse	☐	☐	☐
complex	☐	☐	☐
contract	☐	☐	☐
rate	☐	☐	☐
fluid	☐	☐	☐

Which word did you find most interesting?

_____

© HMH Supplemental Publishers Inc.

NAME _____

READING LONGER WORDS

 You can divide:
- between the words in a compound word.
- after a prefix, or before a suffix.
- between the consonants in a VCCV letter pattern.
- before or after the consonant in a VCV letter pattern.

A. Divide the word. Read each syllable. Then read the whole word.

begin	robot	cubic	music
panic	comic	rapid	robin

B. Divide the word. Read each syllable. Then read the whole word.

reptile	confuse	invite	escape
update	bedtime	online	inside

C. Divide the word. Read each syllable. Then read the whole word.

turnip	target	concert	farther

D. Divide the word. Circle the vowel pair. Read each syllable. Then read the whole word.

elbow	mushroom	shampoo	explain
succeed	window	rainbow	igloo

© HMH Supplemental Publishers Inc.

© HMH Supplemental Publishers Inc.

NAME _____

POEM RUBRIC

When you write a poem, check it against this rubric.

Does your poem express personal feelings and ideas?   Yes ☐   No ☐

	Growth Chart	James's Model	Class Model	My Model
1.	The title gives a clue about the topic of the poem.			
2.	The topic is interesting and makes readers want to read the poem.			
3.	Descriptive words help readers see, hear, smell, taste, and touch the images described.			
4.	The lines in a poem often have a rhythm or pattern.			
5.	The words are chosen carefully so that every word counts.			
6.	A poem can help the reader view the topic, object, or idea in a new way.			
7.	In many poems, the first word in each line begins with a capital letter.			

Score

3. Excellent   2. Good   1. Needs work

NAME _____

WORD MAP

 Poems use descriptive words to help readers picture what they read. A word map can help you think of words and phrases that describe the subject of a poem.

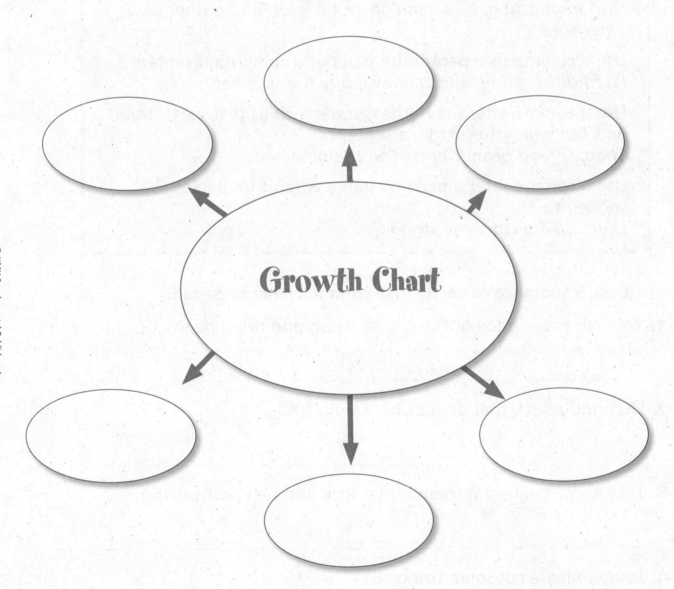

Growth Chart

© HMH Supplemental Publishers Inc.

NAME _____

REVIEW COMMA USE

 Commas tell a reader where to pause. There are several rules for using commas.

Use commas to separate three or more items or steps in a series.
Use a pinecone, peanut butter, birdseed, and string to make a bird feeder.
Find some string, buy some peanut butter, and gather some pinecones.

Use a comma to separate the parts of a compound sentence.
I'll find the string, and Liam will buy the supplies.

Use a comma after time-order words such as *first, next, then,* and *last* when they begin a sentence.
Then, spread peanut butter on the pinecone.

Use a comma after a person's name when that person is spoken to.
Liam, please cut some string.

Write each sentence correctly. Use commas where needed.

1. You can make a toy out of a sock string and dried beans.

_____

2. First find a sock that doesn't have a match.

_____

3. Take some beans put them in the sock and tie it with string.

_____

4. Joseph please cut some string.

_____

© HMH Supplemental Publishers Inc.

NAME _____

EDITING FOR GRAMMAR, SPELLING, AND PUNCTUATION

See also pages 170 and 172.

> ℹ️ A contraction is two words put together to make one word. An apostrophe takes the place of the missing letter or letters.
>
> | | | | | | |
> |---|---|---|---|---|---|
> | *I am* | ⇒ *I'm* | | | *you are* | ⇒ *you're* |
> | *she is* | ⇒ *she's* | *he is* | ⇒ *he's* | *it is* | ⇒ *it's* |
> | *we are* | ⇒ *we're* | | | *they are* | ⇒ *they're* |

> ℹ️ A negative contraction combines a verb with the word *not*.
>
> | | | | |
> |---|---|---|---|
> | *is not* | ⇒ *isn't* | *are not* | ⇒ *aren't* |
> | *was not* | ⇒ *wasn't* | *were not* | ⇒ *weren't* |
> | *does not* | ⇒ *doesn't* | *will not* | ⇒ *won't* |

> ℹ️ A proper noun begins with a capital letter. Only the important words are capitalized.   *the Great Wall of China*

Listen to your teacher. Compare the first draft of the practice paragraph to the edited draft.

A pencil holder is a great Mother's Day or father's day gift. First, get your materials. You need an empty can. Make sure its clean. You also need scissors, glue and magazines. Next, cut out pictures from magazines. Dont use pictures that your mom or dad wouldn't like! Maybe theyre interested in travel. You could find pictures of the Great Pyramids of egypt or the taj mahal in India. Glue the pictures to the can. Finally, let the glue dry.

A pencil holder is a great Mother's Day or Father's Day gift. First, get your materials. You need an empty can. Make sure it's clean. You also need scissors, glue and magazines. Next, cut out pictures from magazines. Don't use pictures that your mom or dad wouldn't like! Maybe they're interested in travel. You could find pictures of the Great Pyramids of Egypt or the Taj Mahal in India. Glue the pictures to the can. Finally, let the glue dry.

© HMH Supplemental Publishers Inc.

NAME _____

READER'S LOG: "PLANTS ARE ALIVE!"

> ℹ️ Active listeners take notes. Active readers do, too. Write only the most important information.

PAIR AND SHARE Reread the selection with your partner. Mark the boxes and take notes as you read. Add to your notes as you talk to your partner.

1. How difficult is the selection?

☐ very difficult   ☐ not too difficult   ☐ easy

2. What makes the selection difficult?

☐ the words   ☐ the information   ☐ everything!

3. List the most difficult words.

_____

4. What did you do about the difficult words?

☐ We talked about them.   ☐ We looked at the pictures.

☐ We looked them up in a dictionary.   ☐ We asked our teacher.

5. How did you use the diagrams? Did they help you?

_____

6. Are there any sentences that you don't understand?

Note the page number, and ask your teacher what they mean. _____

© HMH Supplemental Publishers Inc.

NAME

UNSCRAMBLE THE WORDS

Unscramble each word to spell one of the words in the box. Write the word on the line under the scrambled word.

| INVOLUNTARY | EMOTION | NUTRIENTS | COORDINATE |
| RESPIRATION | | PHOTOSYNTHESIS | |

1. RITTSUNEN (the materials in food that provide energy to plants and animals)

   _____

2. HESSTOSPONYTHI (the way that green plants make their food)

   _____

3. DAOCNIROTE (to make things work together)

   _____

4. NOULVIRNTYA (done without control)

   _____

5. IRROSTEPANI (the process of breathing in and out)

   _____

6. OMTEONI (a strong feeling)

   _____

© HMH Supplemental Publishers Inc.

NAME _____

USE CLUES

Read each sentence. Use context clues to help you figure out the correct vocabulary word from the box to complete each sentence. Write the word on the line.

| rate | characteristics | fluids | complex | network | nerves |

1. The _____ in your body carry messages between the brain and the other parts of your body.

   _____

2. Two _____ of the hummingbird are its long beak and small size.

   _____

3. Clara drinks plenty of _____ when she runs or rides her bike.

   _____

4. Your heart beats at a faster _____ when you run than when you sleep.

   _____

5. Sam did a _____ science experiment that had many steps.

   _____

6. The ants built a _____ of connected tunnels inside the anthill.

   _____

© HMH Supplemental Publishers Inc.

NAME

A. Review

Look at the picture. Read the question. Circle the correct answer.

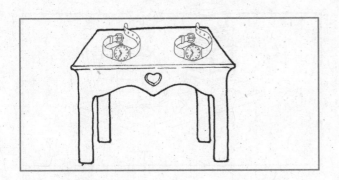

1. Is one watch on the table?

  A Yes, it is.

  B No, two watches are on the table.

  C Yes, I see two watchs.

2. Ari wants to make cookies. What is she doing now?

  A She mixes flour and milk.

  B She has lunch.

  C They mix flour and milk.

3. What is Dad doing?

  A They are riding in the car.

  B It is his car.

  C He is driving his car.

4. What game does Ella play?

  A She plays soccer.

  B They play soccer.

  C She play soccer.

© HMH Supplemental Publishers Inc.

NAME _____

B. Which sentence comes next?

Circle the letter of the BEST sentence to follow the sentence or sentences under each picture.

5. This house belongs to Mr. Brown.

   A It is his house.

   B It is her house.

   C It is my house.

6. Look at my dad's books. What if he puts more books on top?

   A They fell.

   B They fall.

   C They will fall.

PAIR AND SHARE With your partner, discuss something that is owned by more than one person.

Use this sentence frame:

A. Ask a question.

Whose _____ is that? (house, car, bikes)

B. Answer the question.

That is _____. (my parents' house, my brothers' bike, my grandparents' car)

Check page 178 to review how to say that more than one person owns something. Be sure to pronounce the *s'*.

Monitor Language: How's your grammar?

Listen to your partner. Was the correct possessive form used? Was the *s'* pronounced?

Yes, always	Sometimes	Never
☐	☐	☐

© HMH Supplemental Publishers Inc.

NAME

CLOSE READING OF THE TEXT

 Self-monitor your understanding as you read.

1. **Reread.** Start with the last sentences you understood. Then read on from that point.

2. **Take notes.** Write down the most important details. This can help you understand and remember what you read.

3. **Look up words you don't know.**

4. **Ask questions.** Then look for answers to your questions in the text, or you can ask someone.

Informative Text	Notes
The brain has three main parts: 1) The *cerebrum* controls thinking and voluntary movements, such as running. 2) The *brain stem* connects the brain to the spinal cord. It controls involuntary movements, such as breathing air, digesting food, and pumping blood. 3) The *cerebellum* coordinates movements and helps us keep our balance.	Underline anything you do not understand. Take notes. What are the most important ideas? _____ _____ _____ Tell what you reread or a question you asked. _____ _____ _____

© HMH Supplemental Publishers Inc.

© HMH Supplemental Publishers Inc.

NAME _____

READ WITH EXPRESSION

Read the following section aloud. Read with energy and strong emotion. Pause for punctuation marks such as commas, dashes, and periods. Listen to your partner's reading. Then practice the passage a second time.

Note: One slash (/) indicates a short pause for a comma or a dash. Two slashes (//) indicates that you stop for a period or an exclamation point.

> Getting "pumped up" means getting healthy exercise— / and it's good for your heart! // Your heart is a muscle. // Like other muscles, / it does its work when it contracts, / or squeezes together. //
>
> Each time your heart contracts, / blood is pumped through your body. // The flow has a steady rhythm called a pulse. // Your pulse rate is set by your heart. //

NAME

CHECK YOUR UNDERSTANDING

A. Reread "Plants Are Alive!" on **Student Edition** pages 350–359. Then read each sentence below. Circle the letter of the correct answer.

1. A plant needs _____ to make food.

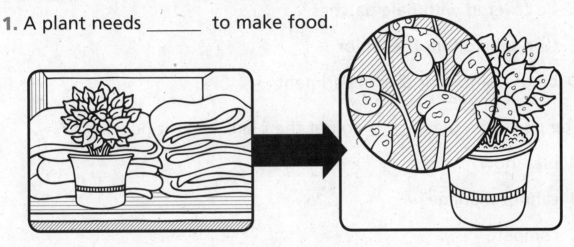

A food coloring

B flowers

C chlorophyll

D attention

2. The plant carried water and nutrients in tiny _____ .

A tubes

B packages

C roots

D cells

© HMH Supplemental Publishers Inc.

NAME _____

B. Read each sentence below. Circle the letter of the correct answer.

3. The leaves of a plant without water will _____ .

   A get dry and wilt

   B be covered with pale patches

   C turn blue or another color

   D be useful for another experiment

4. The parts of a plant _____ to get the plant what it needs.

   A plan how

   B cannot manage

   C compete

   D work together

C. Read each question below. Circle the letter of the correct answer.

5. What are the two jobs of the plant's roots?

   A to carry fluids and nutrients up to the leaves and flowers

   B to hold the plant in place and collect water from the soil

   C to make chlorophyll and food through photosynthesis

   D to find food in the soil and send it up to the leaves and flowers

6. In which direction do nutrients and water travel in a plant?

   A from flowers and leaves down to the roots

   B up the stem to the roots and leaves

   C up the stem from the roots to the leaves and flowers

   D sideways from leaf to leaf

© HMH Supplemental Publishers Inc.

NAME —————————————————————————————————

A. Label

Write a word that names each picture. Use a word from the word box.

write	child	lamb	castle	eight
	chalk	hulk	walk	

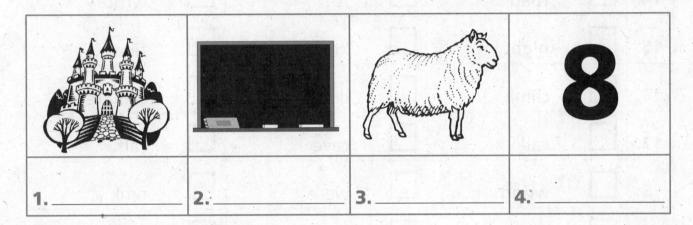

1. _____ 2. _____ 3. _____ 4. _____

B. Listen. Read. Check.

Read these words aloud.

	A	B	C	D	E	F
5.	talk	high	write	path	photo	tiger
6.	chalk	sight	knit	half	cartoon	hatbox
7.	halt	light	knew	wrap	inside	upset
8.	walk	right	knife	wreck	pupil	supper
9.	salt	might	knee	wrong	raincoat	letter
10.	fault	fight	knock	sign	escape	seesaw

C. High-Frequency Words

Read the words aloud.

11.	am	its	now	find	long	down
12.	day	did	get	come	made	part

© HMH Supplemental Publishers Inc.

NAME _____

D. Listen. Read. Check.

Your teacher will say a word. Mark the box next to the word.

13.	☐ knit	☐ night	☐ nine
14.	☐ road	☐ rot	☐ wrote
15.	☐ night	☐ knife	☐ fine
16.	☐ climb	☐ limb	☐ climate
17.	☐ call	☐ cave	☐ calf
18.	☐ wring	☐ were	☐ rank
19.	☐ hate	☐ eat	☐ eight
20.	☐ shy	☐ sigh	☐ sing

E. Spelling

Write the hardest spelling list you can think of. Then test a friend.

21. _____   23. _____

22. _____   24. _____

© HMH Supplemental Publishers Inc.

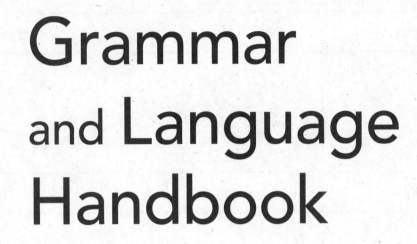

Grammar and Language Handbook

Grammar and Language Handbook

1 What is a noun?

A. A **noun** is a word that names a person, place, or thing.

person	place	thing
boy	park	bus

B. A **noun** can also name an animal.

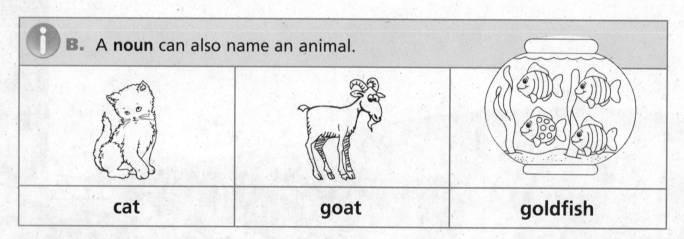

cat	goat	goldfish

C. A **noun** can name an idea, too.

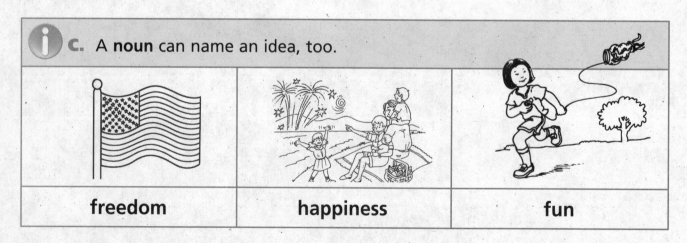

freedom	happiness	fun

© HMH Supplemental Publishers Inc.

2 What are singular and plural nouns?

A. A **singular** noun names one person, place, thing, or animal. A **plural** noun names more than one.

To write the plural of many nouns, add -*s* to the singular noun.

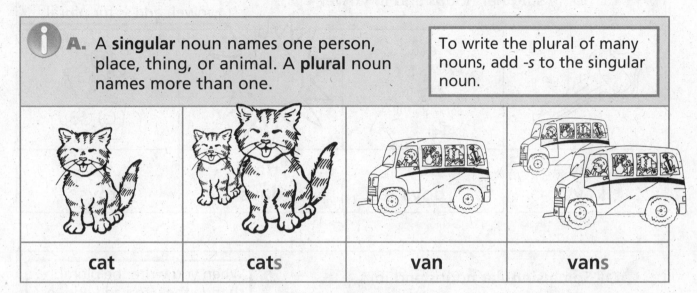

| cat | cats | van | vans |

B. Some **singular** nouns end in *x, ch, tch, sh, zz,* and *ss.*

To write the plural of nouns with these endings, add -*es* to the singular noun.

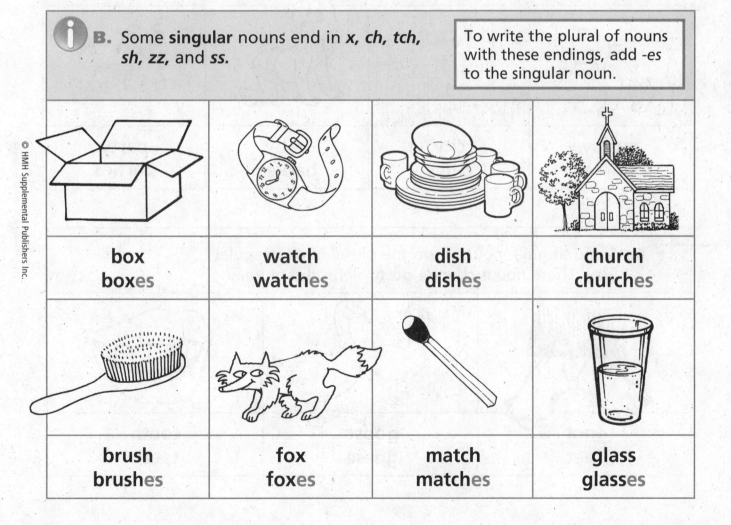

| box boxes | watch watches | dish dishes | church churches |
| brush brushes | fox foxes | match matches | glass glasses |

© HMH Supplemental Publishers Inc.

Grammar and Language Handbook

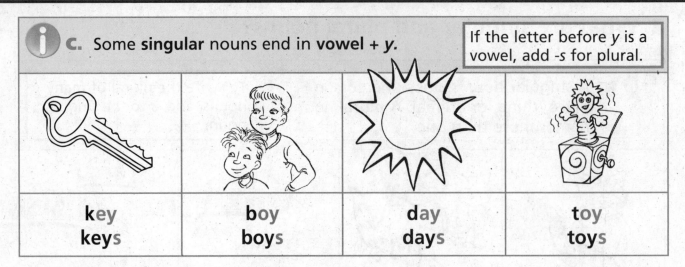

C. Some **singular** nouns end in **vowel + y.**

> If the letter before *y* is a vowel, add *-s* for plural.

key	boy	day	toy
key**s**	boy**s**	day**s**	toy**s**

D. Some **singular** nouns end in **consonant + y.**

> When you write the plural, change the *y* to *i* and add *-es.*

pup**py**	ci**ty**	ba**by**	par**ty**
pupp**ies**	cit**ies**	bab**ies**	part**ies**

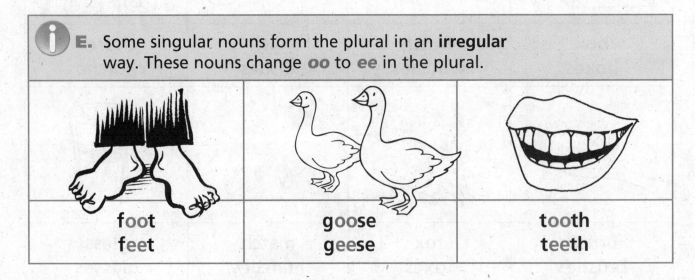

E. Some singular nouns form the plural in an **irregular** way. These nouns change *oo* to *ee* in the plural.

foot	goose	tooth
feet	geese	teeth

© HMH Supplemental Publishers Inc.

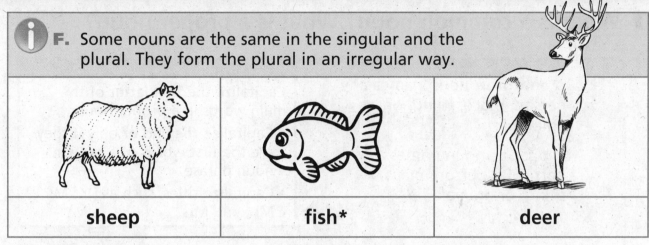

F. Some nouns are the same in the singular and the plural. They form the plural in an irregular way.

sheep	**fish***	**deer**

* The plural of *fish* is sometimes written *fishes*. Both are correct.

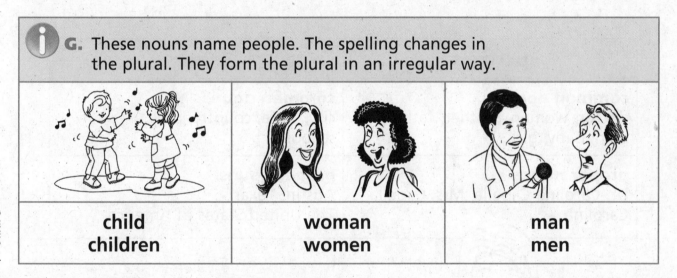

G. These nouns name people. The spelling changes in the plural. They form the plural in an irregular way.

child **children**	**woman** **women**	**man** **men**

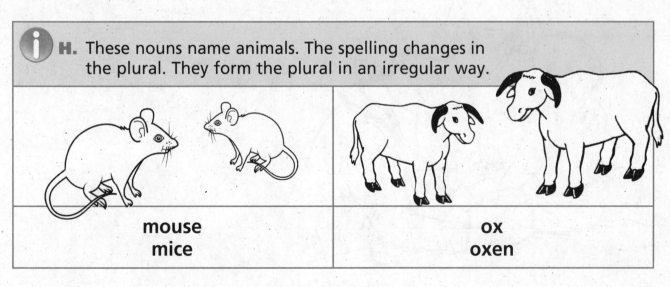

H. These nouns name animals. The spelling changes in the plural. They form the plural in an irregular way.

mouse **mice**	**ox** **oxen**

© HMH Supplemental Publishers Inc.

Grammar and Language Handbook

3 What is a common noun? What is a proper noun?

 A. A **common** noun names any person, place, thing, or animal.

A **proper** noun names a particular person, place, thing, or animal.

Capitalize the **first letter** of the main words in a proper noun.

- Capitalize *the* and *of* only if they are the first words of a proper noun phrase.
- Capitalize **titles**, such as Dr., Ms., Mr., and Mrs.

persons	places
common nouns doctor, woman, mother, father, man, baby, girl	**common nouns** city, state, country, park, school
proper nouns Dr. Carolina Capella, Mrs. Capella, Carolina	**proper nouns** Austin, Texas, The United States of America

© HMH Supplemental Publishers Inc.

Canada

Canada

The United States of America

Texas

Austin

Mexico

Common and proper nouns

things	animals
common nouns book TV show game	**common nouns** dog cat goat
proper nouns Write the names of your favorite shows or games. **?** _____ _____ _____ _____	**proper nouns** names of pets Rufus

B. The words *day* and *month* are common nouns. Specific names of days and months are proper nouns.

> Capitalize the days of the week and months of the year.

November

Sunday	Monday	Tuesday	Wednesday	Thursday	Friday	Saturday
			1	2	3	4
5	6	7	8	9	10	11
12	13	14	15	16	17	18
19	20	21	22	23	24	25
26	27	28	29	30		

© HMH Supplemental Publishers Inc.

Grammar and Language Handbook

4 What is an adjective?

 An **adjective** is a word that describes a noun.

- Adjectives give information about nouns. When we read or listen to others speak, adjectives help us picture the nouns.

- When we speak or write, adjectives are words that help us describe what we see, hear, feel, taste, and smell.

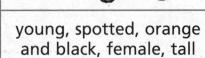

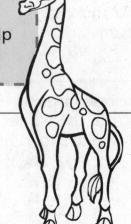

huge, big, gray, mammal, male	small, tiny, little, gray, quick	young, spotted, orange and black, female, tall
 soft, fluffy, cute, white, young	 hard, blue, shiny, metallic	 slimy, brown, wiggly, shiny
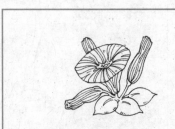 sweet, pretty, colorful, small	 salty, white and yellow, puffy, crunchy	 smelly, greasy!

© HMH Supplemental Publishers Inc.

5 What is a definite article?

There is one definite article in English. It is *the*.
Use *the* before any noun when you have only one
thing in mind.

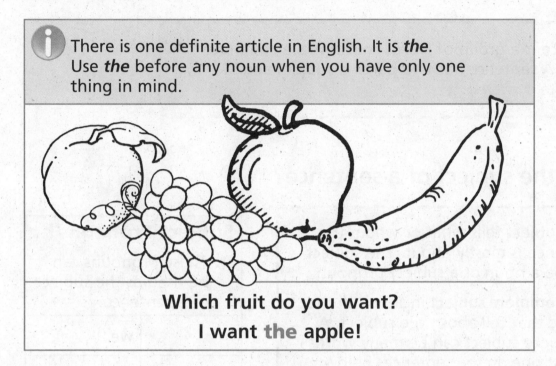

Which fruit do you want?

I want the apple!

6 What are the indefinite articles?

A. There are two indefinite articles: **a** and **an**.

"I want **an** apple!" means "I want **one** apple!"

"I want **a** pear!" means "I want **one** pear!"

You are not definite about which one you want.

B. Use *an* before a word that
starts with a vowel.

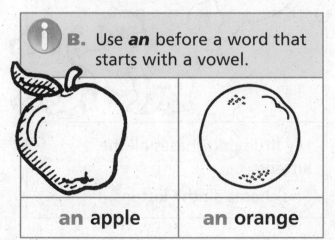

| an apple | an orange |

C. Use *a* before a word that
starts with a consonant.

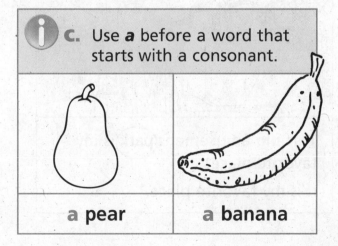

| a pear | a banana |

© HMH Supplemental Publishers Inc.

7 What is a sentence?

A **sentence** is a group of words that forms a complete thought. A sentence has two parts: a **subject** and a **predicate**.

8 What is the subject of a sentence?

A. The **subject** tells what or whom the sentence is mostly about. The subject can be a noun or a subject pronoun.

B. The **complete subject** includes all the words that tell about the subject. A complete subject can be many words or just one. In the sentences below, the complete subject is written in green type.

C. The **simple subject** of a sentence is a noun or a pronoun. In the sentences below, the simple subject is circled.

Subject Pronouns

D. These pronouns can be used as the subject of a sentence.

I	we
you	you
he, she, it	they

This big amusement (park) is my favorite place!

(It) is my favorite place.

My little (dog) chases all the kittens.

(She) chases all the kittens.

© HMH Supplemental Publishers Inc.

9 What is the predicate of a sentence?

A. The **predicate** of a sentence includes the main verb and other words that tell more about the verb. The predicate tells what the subject is, does, or feels.

B. The **complete predicate** includes the verb and other words that tell about the verb. In the sentences below, the complete predicate is written in green type.

C. The **simple predicate** is the verb or verb phrase. In the sentences below, the simple predicate is circled.

© HMH Supplemental Publishers Inc.

The girl kicks the ball hard.

The sad little boy is sitting on the floor.

Grammar and Language Handbook

10 What is a sentence fragment?

 A **fragment** is a group of words that *do not* form a complete thought! Something important is missing in a sentence fragment.

Read these sentence fragments. What questions do you have when you read them?

Fragment	Possible Questions
1. went to the mall	Who did? Why? When?
2. the boy and girl with the rackets	What did they do? When? Where are they going?
3. rode the bike	Who? What? When? Why?

© HMH Supplemental Publishers Inc.

11 What are the four kinds of sentences?

ⓘ	Kinds of Sentences	End Punctuation	Intonation
•	**Statement** (or, declarative)	I finished my homework. **(ends with period)**	Your voice should fall at the end of a statement.
?	**Question** (or, interrogative)	Did you finish your homework? **(ends with a question mark)**	Your voice should rise for a question.
!	**Exclamation** (or, exclamatory)	I did it! **(ends with an exclamation mark)**	Your voice should show excitement for an exclamation.
! or •	**Command** (or, imperative)	Finish your homework now. (!) **(ends with period or an exclamation mark)**	When you make a command, your voice can vary, depending upon how strongly you feel. Ask your teacher to demonstrate.

© HMH Supplemental Publishers Inc.

Grammar and Language Handbook

12 What forms of the verb *to be* should I use?

 A. Present Tense *to be* Use these verbs to tell about noun and pronoun subjects in the present time.

- Omar **is** tired.
- Those girls **are** good students.

I am	We are
You are	You are
He is She is It is	They are

 B. Past Tense *to be* To tell about the subject of a sentence in the past, use the past tense of *to be*. There are only two verbs to remember!

- Omar **was** tired last night.
- Last year, the girls **were** good students.

I was	We were
You were	You were
He was She was It was	They were

 C. Look at the arrows. Nouns and adjectives can follow forms of the verb *to be*. They always tell about the subject.

Present	Past
Omar **is** tired.	Omar **was** tired last night.
Those girls **are** good students.	The girls **were** good students last year.

© HMH Supplemental Publishers Inc.

13 What contractions are made with *am*, *is*, and *are*?

In English, there is a short, quick way to say some common phrases.

The short form is called a **contraction**.

Contractions can be made with pronoun subjects and present tense forms of the verb *to be*.

PAIR AND SHARE: Speaking

Practice with your partner.

Say the first sentence in each section.

Your partner will respond, using the contraction.

Change roles using the next sentence pairs.

Keep practicing!

A.   I am an athlete.
   I'm an athlete.

D.   We are readers.
   We're readers.

B.   You are the best!
   You're the best!

E.   You are all great.
   You're all great.

C.   He is tall.   He's tall.
   She is tall.   She's tall.
   It is tall.   It's tall.

F.   They are tall.
   They're tall.

© HMH Supplemental Publishers Inc.

Grammar and Language Handbook

14 What contractions are made with *not*?

 A. Contractions can be made with the word ***not.***
The word ***not*** makes a sentence negative.

PAIR AND SHARE: Speaking
Practice with your partner.
Say the first sentence in each section.
Your partner will respond, using the contraction.
Change roles using the next sentence pairs.
Keep practicing!

 B. We can form contractions with ***not* + is** and with ***not* + are.**

He is not tall. ⟶ **He isn't tall.**	They are not tall. ⟶ **They aren't tall.**
She is not tall. ⟶ **She isn't tall.**	You are not tall. ⟶ **You aren't tall.**
It is not tall. ⟶ **It isn't tall.**	We are not tall. ⟶ **We aren't tall.**

 C. Contractions can also be made with ***not* + was** and with ***not* + were.**

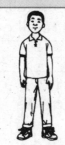  

I was not tall. ⟶ **I wasn't tall.**	We were not tall. ⟶ **We weren't tall.**
He was not tall. ⟶ **He wasn't tall.**	You were not tall. ⟶ **You weren't tall.**
She was not tall. ⟶ **She wasn't tall.**	They were not tall. ⟶ **They weren't tall.**
It was not tall. ⟶ **It wasn't tall.**	

© HMH Supplemental Publishers Inc.

15 What are action verbs?

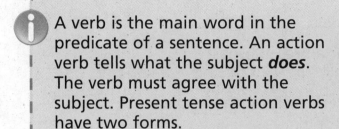

A verb is the main word in the predicate of a sentence. An action verb tells what the subject **does**. The verb must agree with the subject. Present tense action verbs have two forms.

PAIR AND SHARE: Speaking
Practice reading the sentences below the illustrations with your partner.
Pronounce the -s or -es endings in the verbs very clearly.
Your partner should be able to hear the ending in these verbs.
Then change roles.

Agreement Rules for Present Tense Action Verbs

Rule 1 Add -s to most present tense action verbs if the subject is a singular noun or a singular subject pronoun: *he, she, it.*	**Rule 2** Add -es to the present tense verb if it ends in -ch, -tch, -sh, -ss, -x, or -zz and the subject is a singular noun or a singular subject pronoun: *he, she, it.*

Four players **run** to the ball. Julio **gets** there first! He **kicks** the ball. His team **wins**.	The runners **dash** to the finish line. Marta **catches** up. She **passes** them all. She **finishes** first.

© HMH Supplemental Publishers Inc.

16 **What is the correct form of regular action verbs in the past tense?**

In English, the same form is used for all regular past tense verbs.

- When you write, add **-ed** to the verb to form the past tense.

- When you speak, be sure to pronounce the **-ed** ending.

Singular Subject
I work**ed** last night.
John, you work**ed** last night.
The boy work**ed** last night. The girl work**ed** last night. The car work**ed** last night. He, she, and it work**ed** last night.

Plural Subject
We work**ed** last night.
John and Darcy, you both work**ed** last night.
The students work**ed** last night. The dogs work**ed** last night. The cars work**ed** last night. They work**ed** last night.

© HMH Supplemental Publishers Inc.

17 What are common irregular action verbs?

A. The verbs *go, do,* and *have* are irregular in the present tense. They are called *irregular* because we don't *just* add *s* when the subject is a singular noun or *he, she, it.*

B. The verbs *go, do,* and *have* are also irregular in the past tense. The same form is used for all subjects.

Present Tense			
Pronoun Subjects	**Verb**		
	go	**do**	**have**
I, You, We, They	go	do	have
He, She, It	goes	does	has

Past Tense	
to go	went
to do	did
to have	had

Verb *go*	Verb *do*	Verb *have*
We **go** home after school.	We **do** our homework.	We **have** a lot of books.
Kim **goes** home after school.	He **does** his homework on time.	The man **has** a lot of books.
Kim **went** home after school yesterday.	He **did** his homework on time last week.	The man **had** a lot of books before he moved.

© HMH Supplemental Publishers Inc.

18 What are direct objects?

> **A.**
> - **Nouns** that are **direct objects** are affected by the verb.
> - To find the direct object in a sentence, say the verb. Then ask, **What?** or **Whom?**

> **B.** **Direct object pronouns** can replace nouns in a sentence. When you replace a noun that is a direct object, use **them** if the noun is plural. If the noun is singular, use **him, her,** or **it**.

Singular	Plural
me	us
you	you
him, her, it	them

© HMH Supplemental Publishers Inc.

1. My friends feed the ducks.
Feed *what*? **the ducks**
The direct object is **ducks**.

2. My friends feed **them**.
The direct object is **them**.

3. The player kicks the ball.
Kicks *what*? **the ball**
The direct object is **ball**.

4. The player kicks **it**.
The direct object is **it**.

19 How do we show possession or ownership?

 A. English has a special way to show that one person owns something. Use apostrophes!

This cat belongs to Sumi.	The car belongs to my dad.
This cat is **Sumi's**.	The car is my **dad's**.
This is **Sumi's** cat.	It is my **dad's** car.

 B. **When you write,** here's how to show that one person owns something.

When you speak, be sure to pronounce the **s** that follows the apostrophe.

Step 1	Write the noun that names the person.	Sumi	Dad
Step 2	Write an *apostrophe s* after the noun.	Sumi's	Dad's
Step 3	Write what is owned.	Sumi's cat	Dad's car

© HMH Supplemental Publishers Inc.

C. Here's how to show that more than one person owns something.

The bike belongs to the boys. This is the **boys'** bike.	These hoops belong to my sisters. They are my **sisters'** hoops.

 D. When you write, here's how to show that more than one person owns something.

When you speak, be sure to pronounce the *s* ending of the plural noun.

Step 1	Write the noun phrase that names the persons who own something.	**the two boys**	**my sisters**
Step 2	Write an *apostrophe* after the plural noun.	**the two boys'**	**my sisters'**
Step 3	Write what is owned.	**the two boys' bike**	**my sisters' hoops**

© HMH Supplemental Publishers Inc.

© HMH Supplemental Publishers Inc.

 E. You can replace possessive nouns with possessive pronouns.

- Some possessive pronouns come before the noun.
- Some possessive pronouns are not followed by a noun.

other possessive pronouns	
before a noun	**alone**
my bike	mine
your cat	yours
our car	ours

This is the **boys'** bike.
This is **their** bike.
The bike is **theirs**.

They are my **sisters'** hoops.
They are **their** hoops.
The hoops are **theirs**.

This is **Sumi's** cat.
This is **her** cat.
This cat is **hers**.

This is my **dad's** car.
This is **his** car.
This car is **his**.

20 How do we show that something is happening right now?

> **A.** Here are two ways to talk about actions that are happening in the present tense.

B. Use the simple present tense when actions occur regularly or often.	**C.** To show that something is happening right now, use the correct form of *to be* + the *ing* form of the action verb.
Simple Present	**Present Progressive**
1. I **read** every day.	I **am reading** right now.*
2. The girls **sing** a lot.	The girls **are singing** right now.*
3. Celeste always **studies** math.	Celeste **is studying** math right now.*

*In these sentences, *am, are,* and *is* are helping verbs.

© HMH Supplemental Publishers Inc.

21 How do we show that an action will happen in the future?

 A. In English, there is an easy way to show that an action will happen in the future. The magic word is *will.* Just write *will* plus the main verb.

Present Tense	Future Tense
1. I **am studying** hard now.	I **will go** to a great college.
2. You **are** a good student now.	You **will be** a good doctor.
3. He is **not watching** television now.	He **will watch** tonight.

 B. You can form a contraction with subject pronouns and *will.*

I will ➝ I'll	We will ➝ we'll	He will ➝ he'll

 C. To say that something will *not* happen in the future, you can use **will not** or **won't.**

Won't means the opposite of *will.* You can say either:

I *will not* go to bed or I *won't* go to bed.

© HMH Supplemental Publishers Inc.

Grammar and Language Handbook

22 What are negative words in English?

PAIR AND SHARE: Speaking
Study this page with your partner. Then close the book. See how many negative words you can list! Then practice saying sentences, using just one negative word! Try some alternatives with the positive word list.

A. In formal English, use only one negative word in a sentence.

B. What are the negative words?

no	not	never	nobody	nothing	nowhere
isn't	wasn't	weren't	don't	doesn't	won't

C. If you already have one negative in a sentence, you can use *positive* words that are the opposite of the *negative* words.

negative words	never	nobody	nothing	nowhere
positive words	always	somebody anybody	something anything	somewhere anywhere

Not This	Try This
1. I **never** talk to **nobody** in class!	I **never** talk to **anybody** in class. I talk to **nobody** in class.
2. I **didn't** do **nothing**!	I **didn't** do **anything**. I did **nothing**.
3. I **won't** go **nowhere** today!	I **won't** go **anywhere** today. I **will** go **nowhere** today.

© HMH Supplemental Publishers Inc.

23 How can we make our sentences interesting?

 When you write, try making some sentences short. Make some sentences long. Change the way your sentences begin. There are many ways to vary your sentences.

Strategy 1. You can use the **connecting** word *and* to combine different subjects when you write or speak. Be sure to use a plural verb if the subject in the new sentence is plural.

1. A watch **is on the table.**

2. A cell phone **is on the table.**

Write or say: A watch **and** a cell phone **are** on the table.

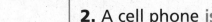

PAIR AND SHARE: Speaking

Find two objects in the same location (under a desk, on the wall).

Say where one object is in a sentence.

Describe where the second object is.

Combine the sentences using *and*.

Use Strategy 1 as the model.

© HMH Supplemental Publishers Inc.

Grammar and Language Handbook

PAIR AND SHARE: Speaking
Name one thing you like in a sentence.
Name one thing you don't like in another sentence.
Combine the sentences using *but*.
Use Strategy 2 as the model.

Strategy 2. When the subject in two sentences is the same, look for differences. If only one sentence has the word *not*, you may be able to combine sentences using the connecting word *but*.

1. I like the watch. | **2.** I do not like the cell phone.

Write or say: I like the watch, but not the cell phone.

Strategy 3. Combine subjects that are different using a pronoun to replace the noun subjects.

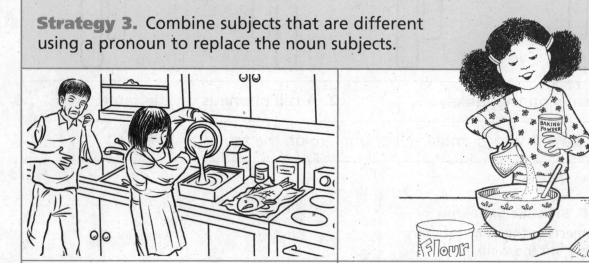

1. My parents are good cooks. (This is a simple subject.)

2. I am a good cook. (This is a simple subject.)

Write or say: My parents and I are good cooks. (This is a compound subject.)
We are good cooks. (This is a simple subject.)

© HMH Supplemental Publishers Inc.

© HMH Supplemental Publishers Inc.

Strategy 4. Use these pairs of conjunctions to combine sentences.

either or
neither nor

PAIR AND SHARE: Speaking

Think of two things you will not do.

Make a statement about one thing in a sentence.

Make another statement about the other.

Combine the sentences using *either or*, or *neither nor*.

Use Strategy 4 as the model.

1. I will not scold my dog.

2. I will not scold my cat.

Write or say: I will not scold **either** my dog **or** my cat.

Or... I will scold **neither** my dog **nor** my cat.

Strategy 5. Some verb forms can be used as adjectives. Look for verb forms ending in *-ed* or *-ing*. See if there are ways to combine sentences using these verb forms.

1. The bees are buzzing.

2. The bees landed on a flower.

Write or say: The **buzzing** bees landed on a flower.

185

Strategy 6. Sometimes it is possible to combine sentences using one of these conjunctions.

after	before	because	when	until

When you combine two sentences using these conjunctions, you often need a comma to separate the two parts of the new sentence.

1. First I eat breakfast.

2. Then I get dressed.

Write or say: After eating breakfast, I get dressed.

Or... Before getting dressed, I eat breakfast.

PAIR AND SHARE: Speaking

Think of two things you do in a certain order.

Write a sentence about each one. (Use words such as *first, next, then* to show the order.)

Combine the two sentences using conjunctions such as *after, before, because, when, until.*

Use Strategy 6 as the model.

© HMH Supplemental Publishers Inc.

Phonics and Spelling Handbook

© HMH Supplemental Publishers Inc.

Phonics and Spelling Handbook

Consonant Letters and Sounds

© HMH Supplemental Publishers Inc.

What is a Consonant?

A consonant is a letter and a speech sound. Consonant sounds are made when some part of the mouth blocks the air when you speak. Your lips, teeth, and tongue can block the air.

PAIR and SHARE: Phonics

Learn a key word that begins with each consonant letter. For example, the letter *f* stands for the sound at the beginning of *fish*.

Use the key word to remind you of the sound this letter stands for.

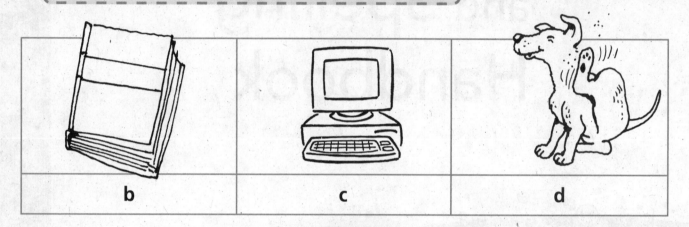

b	c	d

f	g	h

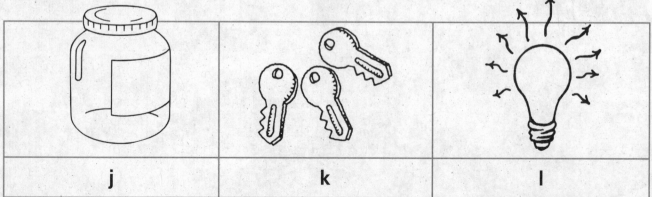

j	k	l

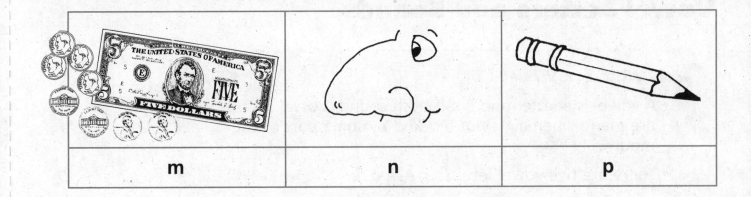

m

n

p

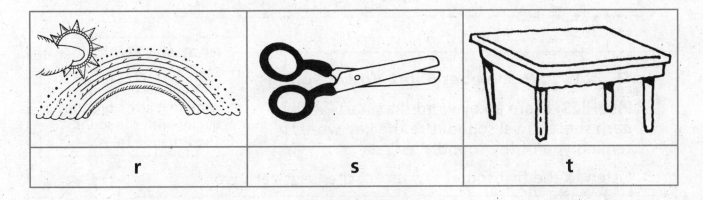

r

s

t

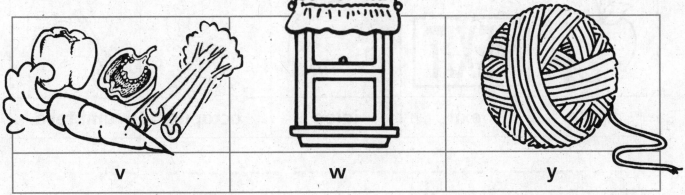

v

w

y

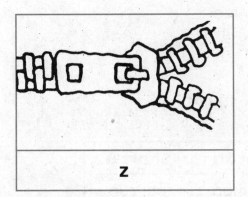

z

PAIR AND SHARE: Spelling

Say a **new word** aloud.

Match the first sounds in the new word and your key word.

Write the letter.

© HMH Supplemental Publishers Inc.

Phonics and Spelling Handbook

Vowel Letters and Sounds

 A. What is a Vowel?

- A vowel is a letter and is a speech sound. Vowel sounds are made when air is *not* blocked by some part of the mouth.

- There are five vowel letters: *a, e, i, o, u.*

- In English, all vowel letters stand for more than one sound.

 B. How to Remember Short Vowel Sounds

PHONICS Learn a key word that starts with each short vowel sound. Use the key word to remind you of the sound.

PAIR and SHARE
Say, *"Short a"* (or *e, i, o, u).* Your partner will name the key word that begins with the sound. Then change roles.

Listen to the first sound as your teacher says each word.

apple	exit	igloo	octopus	umbrella

 C. Letter Patterns in Words with Short Vowel Sounds

PHONICS Look at the word. Answer these questions:

1. Does the word have just one vowel letter?

2. Does the word end in a consonant letter?

If you can answer *yes*, the vowel letter probably stands for a short vowel sound.

Short a	Short e	Short i	Short o	Short u
an, man	Ed, bed	in, pin	on, mop	up, cup

© HMH Supplemental Publishers Inc.

Words with Short Vowel Sounds

PHONICS Reading

Read the slow way. Point to each letter. Say the sound.

Read the fast way. Say the whole word.

Circle a word if you have trouble reading it.

Ask your teacher for help if you need it.

Words with Short *a*

| c a n → can | b a g → bag | r a m → ram | v a n → van |

Words with Short *e*

| j e t → jet | h e n → hen | l e g → leg | w e t → wet |

© HMH Supplemental Publishers Inc.

Words with Short *i*

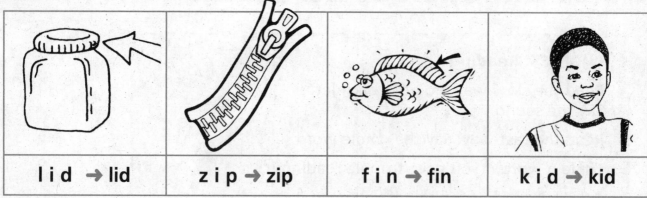

| l i d → lid | z i p → zip | f i n → fin | k i d → kid |

Words with Short *o*

| d o t → dot | m o p → mop | p o t → pot | t o p → top |

Words with Short *u*

| s u n → sun | b u d → bud | s u m → sum | u p → up |

© HMH Supplemental Publishers Inc.

PAIR AND SHARE: Spelling
Say the word aloud.
Say each sound as your partner writes each letter.
Change roles. It's your turn to write a word.
Circle hard words.

Special Consonants

© HMH Supplemental Publishers Inc.

A. The Letter x

The letter *x* stands for more than one sound.
Listen as your teacher reads these words.

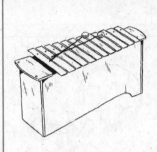

xylophone	x-ray	six	exit

PAIR and SHARE: Phonics
Read each word.
Remember: The letter *x* stands for two sounds!
Listen to your partner read.
Circle hard words.

B. Where x Appears

The letter *x* appears most often at the end of a word or syllable.

Circle the *x* in these words. The letter *x* stands for two sounds: /k/ and /s/. Listen as your teacher reads the words.

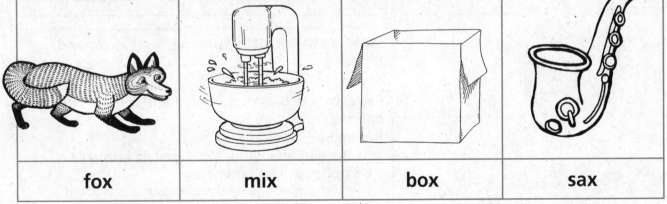

fox	mix	box	sax

193

C. Letters *ck*

The letters *ck* stand for one sound. You will find them at the end of a word or syllable. Listen as your teacher reads the words.

PAIR and SHARE: Phonics
Underline *ck* and *qu* in each word.
Read each word.
Listen to your partner read.
Circle hard words.

duck	pack	sock	kick

 D. Letters *qu*

The letter *q* does not like to be alone! When you see a *q*, look for *u*! Together these letters stand 'for two sounds: /k/ + /w/. Listen as your teacher reads the words. Repeat.

queen	quit	quack	quiet

"QUIET, DUCK!" SAID THE QUEEN.

"QUIT QUACKING!"

PAIR AND SHARE: Spelling final *x*, *ck*, and initial *qu*

Say the word aloud.

Say each sound as your partner writes each letter or letters.

Remember:

- At the end of a word, the sound /k/ is usually written with two letters: *ck*.
- The two sounds /k/ and /w/ together are often written with the letters *qu*.
- When you hear the sounds /k/ /s/ at the end of a word, they may be spelled with an *x*.

Change roles. It's your turn to write a word.

Circle hard words.

© HMH Supplemental Publishers Inc.

E. Double Consonant Letters

Sometimes, words or syllables end in double consonants. The two letters always stand for one consonant sound.

PAIR and SHARE: Reading
Read the word.
Listen to your partner read.
Circle hard words.

			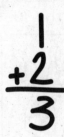
egg	kiss	bell	add

F. Spelling Alert

Read the words above one more time. Many words ending in these sounds are spelled with a single consonant letter. Read the words below. Make sure you know whether the final consonant letter is doubled when you write the word.

l e g → leg	b u s → bus	p a l → pal	d a d → dad

© HMH Supplemental Publishers Inc.

Phonics and Spelling Handbook

Words with Long Vowel Sounds

A. PHONICS Do you know the name of each vowel letter? That is important information because long vowels say their own names. Your teacher will show you what that means.

Learn a key word that starts with each long vowel sound. Use the key word to remind you of the sound this letter stands for.

> **PAIR and SHARE**
> Say, "Long a" (or e, i, o, u). Your partner will name the key word that begins with the sound. Then change roles.

long *a* in *apron*	long *e* in *eat*	long *i* in *ice*	long *o* in *ocean*	long *u* in *united*

B. Letter Pattern: consonant + vowel (as in *me, be, see*)

PHONICS When a vowel letter is at the end of a word or syllable, it usually has a *long* vowel sound. The letter *y* has the same sound as long *i* at the end of a word.

PAIR and SHARE. Read each word. Circle words that are difficult. Practice spelling the word.

Vowel Letters	Words with Long Vowel Sounds
e or ee	be he me we bee see Lee
i or y	hi by my
o	no so go

C. Irregular Words: *do* and *to*

These words *don't* have a long vowel sound! They are irregular. Listen as your teacher reads them.

© HMH Supplemental Publishers Inc.

Vowel Pairs with Long Vowel Sounds

 A. Vowel pairs: *ee and ea*

PHONICS The vowel letters ee stand for the long e sound. In most words, the two letters ea also stand for the long e sound. Circle the vowel pair in each word. Remember, the two vowel letters stand for one vowel sound. Listen as your teacher reads each word.

PAIR and SHARE:
Reading
Read the word.
Listen to your partner read.
Circle hard words.

beet	meal	peel

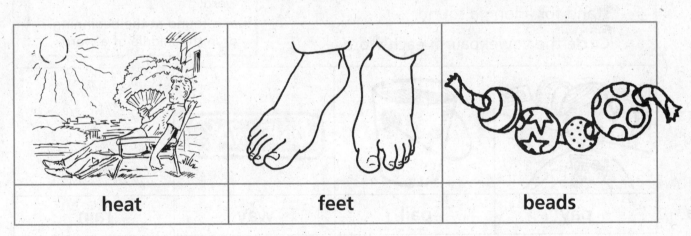

heat	feet	beads

© HMH Supplemental Publishers Inc.

Phonics and Spelling Handbook

Vowel Pairs with Long Vowel Sounds

 B. Vowel pair *oa*

PHONICS The vowel letters *oa* stand for the long *o* sound in most words. Underline the vowel pair in each word. Remember, the two vowel letters stand for one vowel sound. Listen as your teacher reads each word.

PAIR and SHARE: Reading
Read the word.
Listen to your partner read.
Circle hard words.

		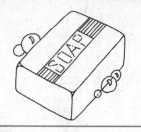	
boat	toad	soap	oak

 C. Vowel pairs *ai* and *ay*

PHONICS The vowel pairs *ai* and *ay* stand for a long *a* sound.

Circle the vowel pair in each word.

SPELLING NOTE:
• *ay* is found at the end of a word.
• *ai* is found at the beginning or in the middle of a word.

pay	pail	way	rain

PAIR and SHARE: Spelling
Long vowel sounds can be spelled in different ways. If you are not sure of the spelling of a word, look it up in a dictionary. Practice spelling the words on this page with your partner.

© HMH Supplemental Publishers Inc.

Long Vowel Letter Pattern: VCe

A. Letter pattern: vowel + consonant + e

PHONICS Look for this letter pattern:
Vowel + Consonant + e

1. The first vowel is long.

2. The final e is silent.

Listen as your teacher reads these words.

c a p e   p i n e   n o t e   c u b e   P e t e

> **SPELLING NOTE:**
> Words with long vowel sounds that end in a consonant can be spelled in several ways. Look up words with these patterns if you are unsure of the spelling.

long *a*	long *i*	long *o*	long *u*	long *e*

c a p e	p i n e	n o t e	c u b e	P e t e

B. READING STRATEGY

1. Does the word end in e? **Circle it.**

2. Does a consonant letter precede the final e? **Check.**

3. Does a vowel letter precede the consonant? **Underline it.**

4. Read the word:

   • The first vowel is long.

   • The final e is silent.

© HMH Supplemental Publishers Inc.

Phonics and Spelling Handbook

Long Vowel Letter Pattern: VCe

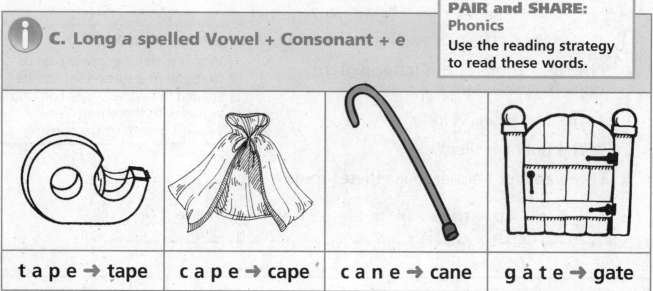

C. Long a spelled Vowel + Consonant + e

PAIR and SHARE:
Phonics
Use the reading strategy
to read these words.

t a p e → tape | c a p e → cape | c a n e → cane | g a t e → gate

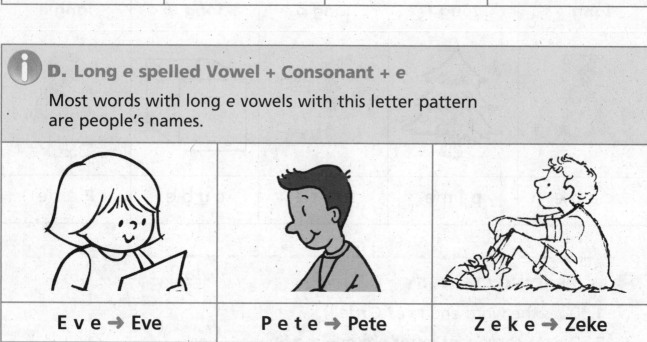

D. Long e spelled Vowel + Consonant + e

Most words with long e vowels with this letter pattern
are people's names.

E v e → Eve | P e t e → Pete | Z e k e → Zeke

PAIR and SHARE: Spelling
Long vowel sounds can be spelled in different
ways. If you are not sure of the spelling of a
word, look it up in a dictionary. Practice spelling
the words on this page with your partner.

© HMH Supplemental Publishers Inc.

ⓘ E. Long *i* spelled Vowel + Consonant + *e*

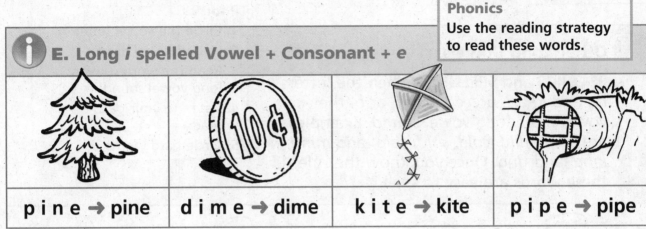

p i n e → **pine**	d i m e → **dime**	k i t e → **kite**	p i p e → **pipe**

ⓘ F. Long *o* spelled Vowel + Consonant + *e*

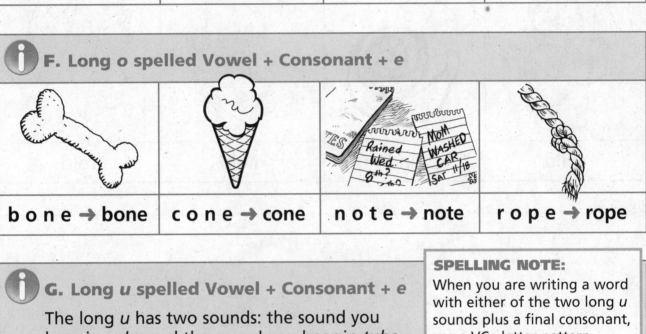

b o n e → **bone**	c o n e → **cone**	n o t e → **note**	r o p e → **rope**

ⓘ G. Long *u* spelled Vowel + Consonant + *e*

The long *u* has two sounds: the sound you hear in *cube* and the sound you hear in *tube*.

SPELLING NOTE:
When you are writing a word with either of the two long *u* sounds plus a final consonant, use a VCe letter pattern.

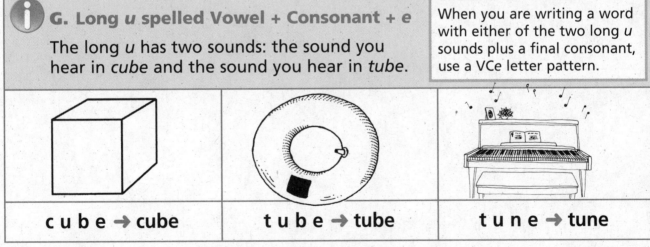

c u b e → **cube**	t u b e → **tube**	t u n e → **tune**

PAIR and SHARE: Spelling
Long vowel sounds can be spelled in different ways. If you are not sure of the spelling of a word, look it up in a dictionary. Practice spelling the words on this page with your partner.

© HMH Supplemental Publishers Inc.

Phonics and Spelling Handbook

Other Long Vowels

PAIR and SHARE:
Phonics
1. **Circle** the vowel letter.
2. **Underline** *nd* or *ld*.
3. **Read** the word using a long vowel sound.
4. **Listen** to your partner read.
5. **Circle** hard words.

 Other Long Vowels

PHONICS and SPELLING When the letters *nd* and *ld* are preceded by *i* or *o*, the vowel has a long vowel sound. Examples are *wild, mild, cold, sold, told,* and *mind, kind,* and *find*. Once you know the rule, these words are easy to spell.

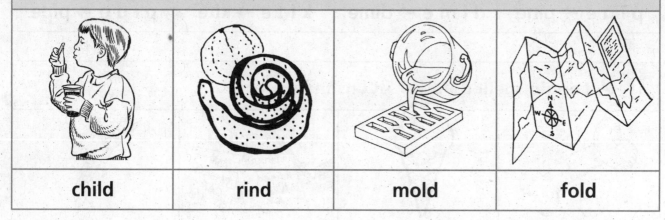

| child | rind | mold | fold |

© HMH Supplemental Publishers Inc.

Two Sounds of *c* and *g*

PAIR and SHARE: Phonics

1. **Circle** the letter *c* or *g*.
2. **Underline** the letter that follows *c* or *g*.
3. **Read** the word.
4. **Listen** to your partner read.
5. **Circle** hard words.

PHONICS NOTES about *c* and *g*

Hard *c* and *g* The letter *c* stands for the sound at the beginning of *computer*. The letter *g* stands for the sound at the beginning of *gate*.

These sounds are called *hard c* and *hard g* sounds.

Soft *c* and *g* When the letters *c* and *g* are followed by *i*, *e*, or *y*, they usually stand for other sounds. Listen as your teacher reads the words below. The letters *c* and *g* are called *soft c* and *g* sounds in these words.

Soft C

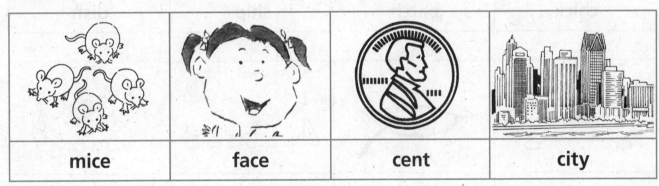

| mice | face | cent | city |

Soft G

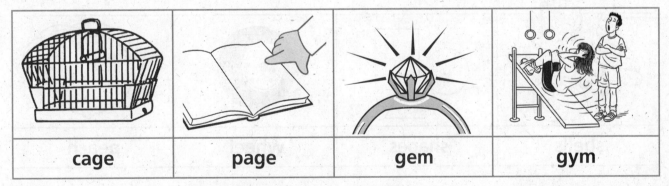

| cage | page | gem | gym |

PAIR and SHARE: Spelling

Be careful!

• Soft *c* as in *cent* can also be spelled with the letter *s*, as in *sent*.

• Soft *g* as in *gem* can also be spelled with the letter *j*, as in *jet*.

If you are unsure of the spelling, look up the word in a dictionary.

© HMH Supplemental Publishers Inc.

Phonics and Spelling Handbook

Consonant Digraphs and Trigraphs

A. Digraphs and Trigraphs *ch, tch, ph, sh, th,* and *wh*

PHONICS These consonant letters stand for just one sound.

PAIR and SHARE: Phonics
Underline the digraph or trigraph.
Read each word.
Listen to your partner read.
Circle hard words.

| chick | patch | ship | dish |

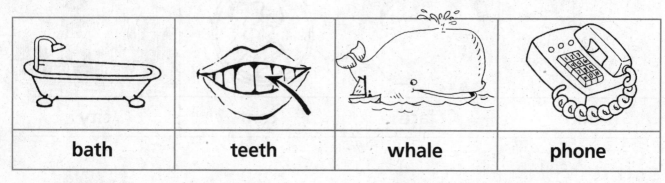

| bath | teeth | whale | phone |

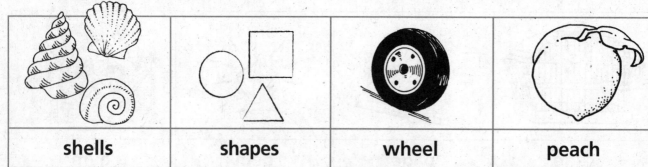

| shells | shapes | wheel | peach |

PAIR and SHARE: Spelling
The sound /ch/ is spelled in two ways: *ch* and *tch*. The spelling *tch* is found only at the end of a word, and *ch* is found at the beginning and end (as in *church*).

© HMH Supplemental Publishers Inc.

© HMH Supplemental Publishers Inc.

B. Digraphs *ng* and *nk*

PHONICS Two other consonant pairs stand for one sound. Listen as your teacher reads the words below.

PAIR and SHARE: Phonics
Underline the digraph.
Read each word.
Listen to your partner read.
Circle hard words.

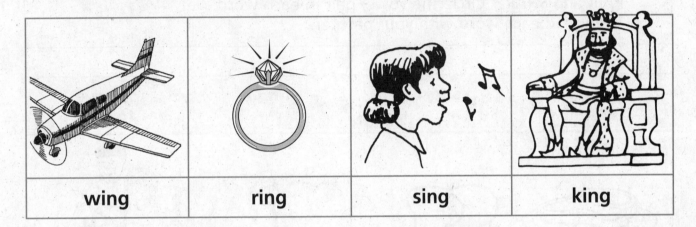

| wing | ring | sing | king |

| sink | tank | skunk | bank |

PAIR and SHARE: Spelling
When spelling one of these words, listen for the /k/ sound at the end of the word. If you hear it, the word ends in *k*, not *g*.

Other Vowel Pairs

 A. Vowel Pair _ea_

PHONICS The vowel pair _ea_ usually stands for the long e sound as in _eat, beads,_ and _heap_. This vowel pair also stands for two other sounds.

Listen as your teacher reads the words below.

PAIR and SHARE Circle the vowel pair in each word. Then read each word with your partner.

> **PAIR and SHARE:**
> **Reading**
> Words spelled with _ea_ can be a challenge to read and spell. Ask your teacher for help or look up the word in the dictionary.

long _a_	short _e_	long _e_	short _e_ long _e_
steak	bread	peak	Today, I read. Yesterday, I read.

long _e_	short _e_	long _e_	long _a_
heat	head	tea	break

© HMH Supplemental Publishers Inc.

206

PHONICS The vowel pair *oo* stands for more than one sound. Listen as your teacher reads the words below.

PAIR and SHARE:
Reading
Underline the vowel pair.
Then read the word.
Listen to your partner read.
Circle hard words.

| moon | spoon | hoot | hoop |

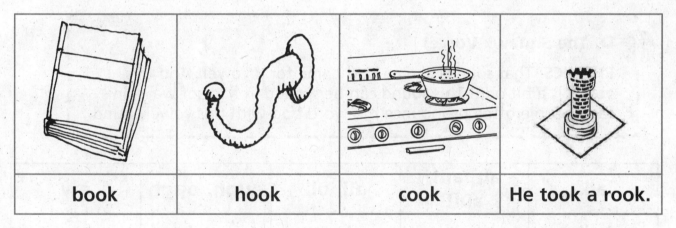

| book | hook | cook | He took a rook. |

© HMH Supplemental Publishers Inc.

PAIR and SHARE: Spelling
Words with the vowel sound in *moon* can be spelled in other ways, as in *dune* and *due*. Look up words with this sound in the dictionary if you are unsure how to spell them.

Phonics and Spelling Handbook

Other Vowel Pairs

PAIR and SHARE:
Reading
Read each word.
Listen to your partner read.
Circle hard words.

 C. Vowel Pairs *ue* and *ew*

PHONICS Long *u* has two sounds: the sound we hear in *cube* and the sound we hear in *tube*. These long *u* sounds can also be spelled with the letters *ue* and *ew*. Listen as your teacher reads each word.

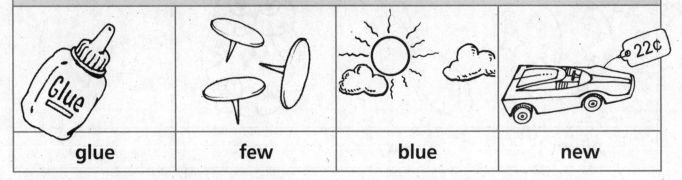

| glue | few | blue | new |

 D. The Squawk Vowel

PHONICS That sounds like an odd name for a vowel! And this vowel is a bit odd! This sound can be spelled in a lot of ways. In fact, people often pronounce the word *dog* with this vowel sound.

alk	alt, aul, ault	all, oll	augh, ough	aw
balk	halt	ball	caught	paw
chalk	malt	call	taught	jaw
talk	salt	fall	bought	law
walk	Paul	mall	sought	raw
	Saul	doll	cough	saw
	fault			
	vault			

PAIR and SHARE: Spelling
Spelling words with vowel pairs can be challenging. Most sounds written with vowel pairs can be spelled in more than one way. Look up the spelling of words with these sounds if you are uncertain.

© HMH Supplemental Publishers Inc.

Diphthongs

 A. Sometimes, a vowel pair stands for two vowel sounds that glide into each other. This kind of vowel pair is called a *diphthong*.

PAIR and SHARE:
Reading

Listen as your teacher reads each word.

Circle the vowel pair.

Read the word. Listen to your partner read.

 B. *oi* and *oy*

PHONICS These letters stand for the same diphthong. Listen as your teacher reads these words.

SPELLING NOTE:

At the end of a word, this diphthong is spelled *oy*. At the beginning or middle of a word, it is spelled *oi*.

| oink | toy | soil | coin |

 C. *ou*

The letters *ou* can stand for the vowel sounds in *you*, *youth*, and *your*. These letters often stand for a diphthong, as in the words below.

SPELLING NOTE:

The *ou* diphthong can also be spelled with the letters *ow*, as in *cow*. Look up words with this sound if you are unsure of the spelling.

 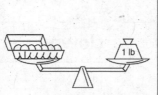  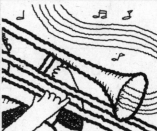

| hound | pound | ground | sound |

© HMH Supplemental Publishers Inc.

Phonics and Spelling Handbook

Diphthongs

 D. *ow*

PHONICS When the letter *w* is at the end of a word or syllable, it acts like a vowel. The letters *ow* are a vowel pair.

• These letters stand for the long vowel sound we hear in *crow*.

• They also stand for the diphthong we hear in *cow*.

There are no rules to use for pronouncing words spelled with *ow*.

PAIR and SHARE:
Reading

Listen as your teacher reads each word.

Practice reading these words with your partner.

Look up the pronunciation of a word if you are not sure of the spelling.

crow	snow	cow	crown
bowl	mow	clown	howl

PAIR and SHARE: Spelling
The diphthong *ow* in *cow* is sometimes spelled in other words with *ou* (as in *round*). If you don't know how to spell a word with this sound, look it up.

© HMH Supplemental Publishers Inc.

Vowels + *r*

PAIR and SHARE:
Reading

Listen as your teacher reads each word.

Repeat the word.
Listen to your partner read.

 A. Vowels + *r*

PHONICS When the letter *r* follows a vowel, it can change the usual sound of the vowel.

 B. *a + r*

PHONICS When followed by *r*, or *r* + a consonant, the letter *a* has the same sound that it does in words such as *pa*, *ma*, and *watch*.
Read these words.

		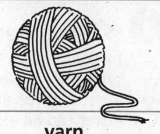
car	**star**	**yarn**

 C. *or*, *oar*, *ore*

PHONICS In words spelled *or*, *oar*, and *ore*, the letter *r* changes the vowel sound. Read each word.

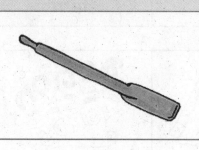		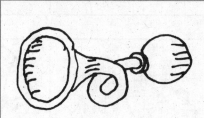
oar	**core**	**horn**

© HMH Supplemental Publishers Inc.

211

Phonics and Spelling Handbook

C. Exceptions

PHONICS In these words, you can hear the long vowel sound even though the letter *r* follows it.

steer	**pair**	**fire**

PAIR and SHARE: Reading

Listen as your teacher reads each word.

Practice reading these words with your partner.

Note: some other words with these spellings may be pronounced differently. For example, *word* is not pronounced like *ford*.

Check the pronunciation of words with these letter patterns in a dictionary.

D. Vowels Combined with *r*

PHONICS AND SPELLING In these words, the vowel combines with the *r*. Listen as your teacher reads each word. The vowel + *r* stands for the same in all of these words, but the vowel letter can be *e*, *i*, *o*, or *u*. That makes spelling difficult!

bird	**fir**	**fur**	**fern**

herd	**shirt**	**skirt**	**words**

PAIR and SHARE: Spelling

Words with one of the vowel letters *i*, *u*, *e*, or *o* that is followed by the letter *r* may all sound alike. Look up the spelling of these words in a dictionary if you are not sure which vowel letter to use.

© HMH Supplemental Publishers Inc.

Silent Letters

© HMH Supplemental Publishers Inc.

> ### ⓘ Silent Letters
>
> Some letters in English are silent. They can make reading *and* spelling difficult! Getting to know which letters are likely to be silent will help you. Look up words if you are unsure of the spelling or pronunciation. You can also search online for silent letters in English.

Silent Letters	Example Words				
b	numb	comb	lamb	climb	crumb
g	sign				
gh	eight	thought	straight	height	light	right
k	know	knew	knit	knock	knee	knife
l	calf	half	talk	walk	would	should
t	castle	fasten	whistle			
w	wrap	write	wrote	written	wreck	wrong

Phonics and Spelling Handbook

PHONOLOGY: CONSONANT BLENDS WITH /S/

A. Initial Blends with _s_

When a word begins with _s_ + one or more consonant letters, be sure to pronounce all consonant sounds.

Practice with these words. Make a difference in how the words in each group sound.

sip, slip, skip	soup, stoop, sloop	sell, smell, spell
side, slide, snide	Sam, slam, scam	seep, steep, sleep
sub, snub, stub	sat, scat, slat	sop, stop, slop

B. Final Blends with _s_

When a word ends with _s_ + one or more consonant letters, make sure you pronounce all of the consonant sounds. Say each consonant sound in the order it occurs in the word.

Practice with these words. Make a difference in how the words in each group sound.

lass, last, lasts	Tess, test, tests	less, lest, let's
mass, mast, masts	miss, mist, mists	Wes, west, wets
lap, laps, lapse	loss, lost, lots	Gus, gust, gusts

© HMH Supplemental Publishers Inc.

PHONOLOGY: CONSONANT BLENDS WITH /S/

C. Ask

When you say the word *ask*, pronounce it so that it sounds different from the word *ax*. The word *ask* rhymes with *task, mask,* and *bask*.

D. Word Sort

Which words have /sk/ sounds? Which words have /ks/ sounds? Write words in the first row that end in /sk/ sounds.

Write words in the second row that end in /ks/ sounds.

task	mask	tax
max	backs	ask
desk	oaks	risk

Row 1: /sk/ _____

Row 2: /ks/ _____

Practice reading these sentences. Pay close attention to how you pronounce the colored letters.

1. I have pins and tacks.

2. Did you wear that mask?

3. Did you ask me a question?

4. Can you move those desks?

5. He asked me politely!

© HMH Supplemental Publishers Inc.

Phonics and Spelling Handbook

PHONOLOGY: CONSONANT BLENDS WITH /S/

E. Other Initial Blends

Some words begin with three consonants, as in *strong*. Some begin with one single consonant and a consonant digraph, as in *shrink*. Be sure to pronounce all consonant sounds in the order they occur in the word.

Practice with these words.

stream, scream	strap, scrap	stroll, scroll
shrimp, scrimp	shrub, scrub	shriek, screech

F. Other Final Blends

Make sure you pronounce all of the consonant sounds in a word. Say each consonant sound in the order it occurs.

Practice with these words. Make a difference in how the words in each group sound.

1.	rap, raps, rapt	pack, pact, packs	men, mend, mends
2.	an, and, hands	fine, find, finds	give, gift, gifts
3.	chip, chimp, chimps	pick, pink, ping	kick, kink, king
4.	putt, punt, punts	set, sent, sends	truck, trunk, trunks
5.	lit, lift, lifts	correct, corrected	land, lands, landing

© HMH Supplemental Publishers Inc.

LEARNING STRATEGIES

You are learning English in so many ways! Check the boxes to show how much progress you've made. Check all boxes that apply.

- ☐ I pronounce English words better than I did before.

- ☐ I can spell correctly.

- ☐ I use new words when I speak.

- ☐ I use new words in my writing.

- ☐ I use pictures, charts, graphs, and maps to help me understand words.

- ☐ When I see or hear an unfamiliar word or expression, I'm better at figuring out its meaning.

- ☐ I know much more about English grammar.

- ☐ I know how to speak to teachers and adults, and how to speak to my friends.

- ☐ I ask for help when I don't understand.

- ☐ I've gotten better at recognizing and correcting mistakes in my writing.

© HMH Supplemental Publishers Inc.

I'M LISTENING!

Check the boxes to show the ways you have become a better listener. Check all boxes that apply.

- ☐ I know which letters stand for sounds in words that I hear.

- ☐ I watch people's gestures and expressions to help me understand spoken English.

- ☐ I understand more of what I see and hear in newspapers and magazines, and on television, radio, and the Internet.

- ☐ I understand more of what people say about topics I already know.

- ☐ I understand more of what people say about topics I don't already know.

- ☐ I take notes to help me understand spoken English.

- ☐ I'm better at answering questions about stories and information that I hear.

- ☐ I understand more of my teacher's directions, and I can repeat them.

- ☐ When people speak, I understand faster and better than I did before.

© HMH Supplemental Publishers Inc.

SAY IT ALOUD

Check the boxes to show the ways you have become a better speaker. Check all boxes that apply.

☐ I know how to pronounce words better than I did before.

☐ I can describe people, places, and things better than I could before.

☐ I can use both simple and complex sentences when I speak.

☐ I use vocabulary words correctly when I speak.

☐ I can share information with my classmates when we work together.

☐ I know how to ask for help when I need it.

☐ I'm better at expressing ideas, opinions, and feelings.

☐ I can tell about events better than I could before.

☐ I'm better at retelling stories that I have read.

☐ I know how to speak to teachers and adults and how to speak to my friends.

© HMH Supplemental Publishers Inc.

Check Your Progress

READ IT!

Check the boxes to show the ways you have become a better reader. Check all boxes that apply.

☐ I know how to read more words, including longer words.

☐ I recognize more high-frequency words than I did before.

☐ I understand more of the words that I see around me at school, at home, and in my town.

☐ I use pictures to help me understand what I read.

☐ I can use what I already know to understand new topics.

☐ I can use information from classroom discussions to help me understand reading selections.

☐ If I don't know a word, I can figure out the meaning by looking at nearby words and sentences.

☐ I can talk about and retell reading selections better than I could before.

☐ I ask for help from my classmates and teacher when I don't understand.

☐ I can take notes about reading selections.

☐ I can answer questions about reading selections.

☐ I read better, faster, and with greater understanding than I did before.

© HMH Supplemental Publishers Inc.

Check Your Progress

WRITE IT!

Check the boxes to show the ways you have become a better writer. Check all boxes that apply.

☐ I'm better at spelling high-frequency words than I was before.

☐ I use high-frequency words correctly in my writing.

☐ I'm better at using spelling rules to write new words.

☐ I use vocabulary words correctly in my writing.

☐ I use a variety of sentence types and lengths when I write.

☐ I'm better at applying grammar rules in my writing.

☐ I can edit my writing to correct mistakes and make it better.

☐ I can describe events in writing better than I could before.

☐ I'm better at giving information in writing.

☐ I'm better at expressing ideas in writing.

☐ I can write better and faster than I could before.

© HMH Supplemental Publishers Inc.

Index for Handbooks

GRAMMAR and LANGUAGE HANDBOOK

Adjectives	164
Articles	165
Conjunctions	184–186
Contractions	171
with *to be* (present)	171
with *not*	172
with *was* and *were*	172
with *will*	181
with *will not*	181
Negative Words	182
Contractions with *not*	181
Negative words	182
Use of positive words	182
Nouns	158
Definition	158
Common and proper	162–163
Singular and plural	159
• Add –*s*	159
• Add –*es*	159
• Ending in *y*	160
• Irregular	160–161
Possessives	177
Plural nouns	178
Pronoun + noun	179
Singular nouns	177
Stand-alone pronouns	179
Pronouns	See below
Interrogative	169
Object	176
Possessive	179
Subject	166
Sentences	166
Definition	166
Fragment	168
Intonation	169
Kinds of sentences	169
Predicate of	167
Punctuation	169
Subject of	166
Subject pronouns	166
Sentence Combining	183
Combine subjects	183
Using *and*	183, 184
Using *but*	184
Using *either, neither*	185
Correlative conjunctions	186
Simple predicates	184
Using participles	185
Using pronouns	184
in complex sentences	186

Verbs: action	173
Agreement: present	173
Formation: past tense	174
Irregular	175
Simple present tense	180
Present progressive	180
Future tense	181
Verbs: *to be*	170
Present tense	170
Agreement	170
Past tense forms	170
Contractions: *am, is, are*	171
Contractions: *was, were*	172

PHONICS and SPELLING HANDBOOK

Consonants	188
Single	188–189
Special consonants	193
Consonant *x*	193
Consonants *ck, qu*	194
Double final	195
Soft *c* and soft *g*	203
Digraphs and Trigraphs	204
Digraphs *ng, nk*	205
Vowels: Short	190
Short vowels	190
Words with short *a, e*	191
Words with short *i, o, u*	192
Vowels: Long	196
Spelled CV, CVV	196
Vowel pairs *ee, ea*	197
Variable *ea*	206
Vowel pairs *oa, ay, ai*	198
VCe letter pattern	199
VCe strategy	199
aCe, eCe	200
iCe, oCe, uCe	201
Vowel lengthened	202
Vowel pairs *ew, ue*	208
Vowels (variable)	207
oo	207
Squawk	208
Diphthong *oi, oy*	209
Diphthong *ou*	209
ow (diphthong, long *o*)	210
Vowels + *r*	211
a + r	211
*oar, ore, or*C	211
Exceptions	212
Vowels combined with *r*	212
Silent Letters	213

© HMH Supplemental Publishers Inc.

Standardized
Test Practice

Standardized Test-Taking Tips

Cut out the tips below and use them with the Standardized Test Practice.

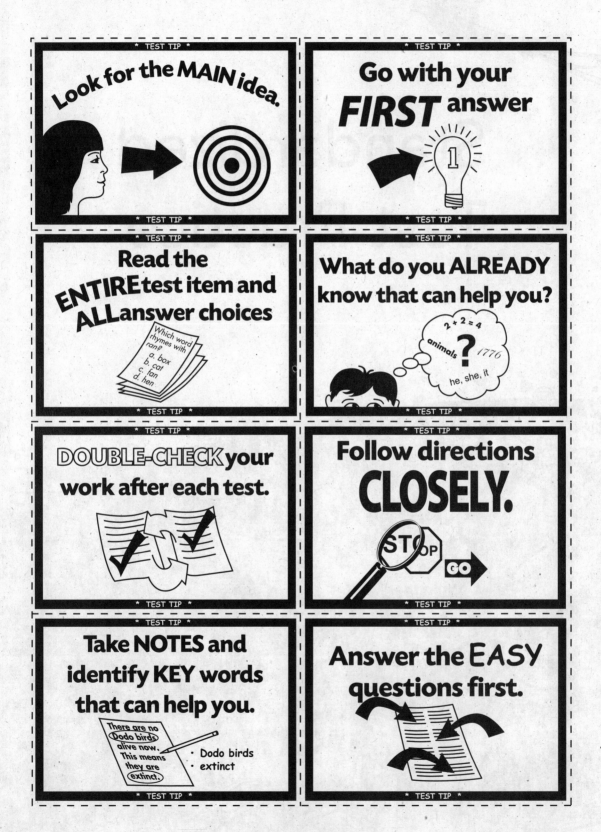

© HMH Supplemental Publishers Inc.

Practice Test 1

> **Read these two selections. Then answer the questions that follow them.**
> **Fill in the circle of the correct answer on your answer document.**

An Unexpected Adventure

1   Selena raced downstairs. "Mom," she cried, "Cassie invited me to her party next weekend. I've *always* wanted to go to one of her parties!"

2   Selena's mother placed her hand on Selena's shoulder. "Remember that we are visiting your cousins in Florida next weekend. You haven't seen them since you were young, and they are excited to see you."

3   Selena's cheeks turned red. "But, Mom, I HAVE to go. Why don't you, Dad, and Rick go without me? I could stay with Grandma."

4   "No, Selena," her mom said sternly. "There will be other parties."

5   On the drive to Florida, Selena's little brother Rick couldn't stop talking about meeting their cousins Kim and Mark. They were the same age as Selena and Rick. Rick just knew they would have lots of fun together. Rick's chattering annoyed Selena. She was determined not to have fun. How could hanging out with the cousins be more fun than Cassie's party?

6   The cousins lived right on the coast. When Selena's family arrived, Kim answered the door. "Welcome!" she said. "We have been looking forward to your visit. Selena, it is so nice to have you here!"

7   "Hi, Kim," said Selena half-heartedly. "I'm happy to be here, too," she lied.

8   At that very moment, Mark came running up. "Quick! Come with me!" he shouted. "I found something on the beach."

9   The four kids rushed to the beach and found a large animal struggling in the sand. "What is it? It looks like it's hurt. What should we do?" cried Rick.

10   "It's a manatee," Kim explained. "It may have been hit by a boat." She took out her cell phone and dialed 911 to report the injured animal.

11   Thoughts about Cassie's party vanished like a puddle on a hot day. Selena had never seen a manatee before. Now she was just a few inches away from one! It was huge—about 10 feet long—with smooth skin. It looked like a walrus without tusks. It had a wide body and sweet face.

GO ON

© HMH Supplemental Publishers Inc.

12   Within minutes, a rescue team arrived. They hoisted the manatee onto a stretcher and examined it. The team leader turned to the kids. "Good work! A boat struck this manatee, but your quick response helped to save its life. We'll take it to our lab where we can treat the injuries."

13   "Can't you treat it here so that we can watch?" asked Rick.

14   The rescuer tousled Rick's hair. "I'm afraid not. I'll tell you what, though. Why don't you all come to the lab tomorrow to visit him. We'll make all of you members of the Junior Rescue Team!"

15   Selena smiled as she thought to herself, "Mom was right. I *am* enjoying this trip. Rescuing a manatee with my cousins in Florida is really exciting, and there will be other parties when I get back home."

16   Rick and Mark beamed with pride. Selena turned to Kim and exclaimed, "You are amazing—a true manatee heroine! I can't wait to tell my friend Cassie all about what happened and our thrilling adventure."

Mermaids of the Coast

1   *The day before, when the Admiral was going to the Rio del Oro, he said he saw three mermaids who came quite high out of the water but were not as pretty as they are depicted, for somehow in the face they look like men.*

— From the diary of Christopher Columbus, January 9, 1493

2   In folk tales, mermaids are half human and half fish. Long ago, sailors claimed they saw mermaids. What they probably saw were manatees. These large sea animals have long, wide bodies. They grow up to 13 feet long and look like fat torpedoes. They can weigh over 2,000 pounds. Manatees are also called "sea cows" because they eat plants. They can eat up to 150 pounds of seagrass and other plants each day.

3   Manatees live in warm waters along the coast. In the United States, they live mainly along the coast of Florida. They can also be found off the coast of Texas in the Gulf of Mexico and as far north as Virginia.

4   Manatees are gentle animals, but their population is threatened. The chief threats to manatees in the U.S. are pollution and boats.

© HMH Supplemental Publishers Inc.

GO ON →

5 Manatees are slow swimmers, so they have little protection from speeding boats. A manatee can become seriously injured or die if a boat hits it. Boat <u>collisions</u> are the leading cause of death to manatees in Florida.

6 Garbage, sewage, chemicals, and oil spills also put manatees at risk. These things harm the plants manatees eat. The manatees can become sick or die. The year 1996 was the deadliest for Florida's manatees. Pollution caused toxic algae to grow in the water. That year, 151 manatees died.

7 It is important to protect manatees. Why? They eat plants and keep waterways clear. Too many plants can clog waterways and harm reefs. Protecting manatees makes the quality of the water better for people. Manatees should also be preserved because they are unique.

8 In 1978, lawmakers passed the "Florida Manatee Sanctuary Act." It made the entire state a safer place for manatees. Boats must travel only in certain areas. They also must travel at slow speeds. Any person who harms a manatee must pay a fine.

9 Everyone can help protect manatees. Here are some tips:

10 • **When boating:** Be on the lookout for manatees in the water and stay at least 50 feet away. Be sure to obey boating speed limits.

• **When swimming or diving:** Look, but don't touch! Feeding manatees could encourage them to swim to people who might harm them.

• **When visiting beaches:** Do not throw garbage on beaches or in the water. Put it in a proper container or recycle it if you can.

• **When spotting an injured manatee:** Call 911 or your local Fish and Wildlife Service immediately. A rescue team will come to help.

11 You can become involved. Learn about manatees. Join a group that cleans beaches or supports manatee rescue. You can even "adopt" a manatee. When we protect the "mermaids of the coast," we are helping ourselves.

© HMH Supplemental Publishers Inc.

Use "An Unexpected Adventure" (pp. 225–226) to answer questions 1–11.

1 Which choice **BEST** describes the main conflict in the story?

A Cassie's party and the trip are on the same weekend.
B Cassie does not like Selena.
C Selena's mother won't let Selena stay with her grandmother.
D Selena is annoyed with Rick.

2 In paragraph 3, Selena's cheeks "turned red" to show that Selena is —

F embarrassed
G running
H upset
J thrilled

3 Before leaving for Florida, Selena's attitude toward her mother is —

A resentful and disobedient
B gentle and loving
C delighted, but defiant
D respectful, but disappointed

4 Paragraph 5 is mainly about —

F Selena's disappointment
G the drive to Florida
H Selena meeting her cousin
J finding a manatee

5 Look at this diagram of information from the story.

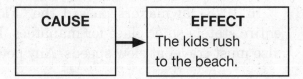

Which of the following belongs in the empty box?

A Kim answers the door.
B Mark finds something on the beach.
C Selena lies to Kim.
D Rick annoys Selena.

GO ON

© HMH Supplemental Publishers Inc.

6 In paragraph 7, why does Selena lie to Kim?

    F Selena is resentful toward Kim.
    G Selena is selfish.
    H Selena's mother would be angry.
    J Selena doesn't want to hurt Kim's feelings.

7 In paragraph 11, the author writes that thoughts of the party vanished "like a puddle on a hot day" to show that —

    A Selena will not have fun in Florida
    B Selena still wants to go to the party
    C Selena is not thinking about the party anymore
    D Cassie has cancelled the party

8 In paragraph 14, an antonym of the word <u>tousled</u> is —

    F cleaned
    G messed
    H pulled
    J straightened

9 Selena stopped thinking about Cassie's party because she was —

    A distracted by the injured manatee
    B angry she didn't have a cell phone
    C sure Cassie would never invite her again
    D angry at Mark for making them go to the beach

10 Selena told Kim she was amazing because she —

    F saw that Kim was eager to visit
    G was envious of Kim's cell phone
    H admired Kim for acting to save the manatee
    J realized that living in Florida was great

11 At the end of the story, the reader can predict that Selena —

    A is anxious to return home
    B will enjoy the rest of her visit with her cousins
    C is afraid of manatees
    D will never speak to Cassie again

© HMH Supplemental Publishers Inc.

GO ON ➡

Use "Mermaids of the Coast" (pp. 226–227) to answer questions 12–18.

---

12 Why does the author use a quotation from Columbus's diary?

   F To prove that manatees are mermaids

   G To persuade the reader to save manatees

   H To explain what life was like for the Admiral

   J To show that sailors once thought manatees were mermaids

13 This article is mainly about —

   A sailors of long ago

   B pollution

   C protecting manatees

   D boating

14 Which words in paragraph 5 help the reader know the meaning of <u>collisions</u>?

   F *in harm's way*

   G *seriously injured or die*

   H *if a boat hits it*

   J *leading cause of death*

15 Which of the following is **NOT** a way to help protect manatees?

   A feed manatees when you see them

   B obey boating speed rules

   C reduce water pollution

   D support manatee rescue operations

© HMH Supplemental Publishers Inc.

GO ON

16 Look at this diagram of information from the story.

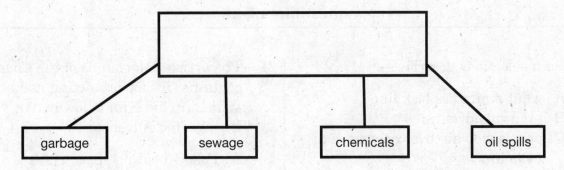

Which idea belongs in the empty box?

F How to Protect Manatees
G Types of Toxic Algae
H Living Spaces of Manatees
J Examples of Pollution

17 What caused so many manatees to die in 1996?

A Oil spills
B Toxic algae
C Collisions with boats
D Hunting by humans

18 From information in the selection, the reader can determine that manatees —

F are a nuisance to people
G are harmful to waterways
H need protection
J are better protected in other countries

© HMH Supplemental Publishers Inc.

GO ON

Use "An Unexpected Adventure" and "Mermaids of the Coast" to answer questions 19–21.

19 Both selections describe —

   A what manatees look like

   B exciting adventures

   C people who discover new ways to have fun

   D children who save a manatee

20 One idea that can be found in both selections is that —

   F people cause pollution

   G family is important

   H it is important to report an injured animal

   J protecting the environment harms people

21 The article "Mermaids of the Coast" contains tips for protecting manatees. Which tip did Kim follow in "An Unexpected Adventure"?

   A Follow boating speed rules.

   B Call 911 or your local Fish and Wildlife Service immediately.

   C Stay at least 50 feet away from the animal.

   D Do not throw garbage on beaches.

© HMH Supplemental Publishers Inc.

GO ON

> Read this selection. Then answer the questions that follow it.
> Fill in the circle of the correct answer on your answer document.

Dr. Hector P. Garcia: Justice for One and All

1   Dr. Hector Garcia was a remarkable man. He was a doctor, a war hero, and a defender of Mexican-American rights.

2   In 1917, there was a violent war in Mexico. Dr. Garcia's family fled Mexico and moved to the small town of Mercedes in south Texas. Although his parents had both been teachers in Mexico, their education was not recognized in Texas. Many people in Texas treated Mexican-Americans poorly. The Garcia family witnessed violence and injustice firsthand. They also experienced poverty.

The Struggle for Education

3   Mr. and Mrs. Garcia encouraged their children to succeed by means of education, but the road to Hector's medical degree was not easy. One high school teacher told him, "No Mexican will ever get an 'A' in my class." Despite the challenges, Hector succeeded in high school and then earned a degree at Edinburgh Junior College. He hitchhiked 30 miles every day just to get there!

4   In 1940, Hector received his medical degree at The University of Texas at Galveston. This was quite an accomplishment. At that time, the school would admit only one Mexican-American student each year.

A War Hero Returns Home

5   During World War II, Dr. Garcia enlisted in the U.S. Army. He earned the rank of Major and was awarded several medals. After the war, he settled in Corpus Christi with his wife and daughter. He opened a medical practice, but he did not forget his roots.

6   Mexican-Americans still struggled. Poverty and discrimination were rampant. Mexican-Americans were not allowed in many restaurants, theaters, swimming pools, and clubs. Mexican-American farm workers lived in inhuman conditions. Many disabled Mexican-American veterans who served during World War II were starving and sick.

© HMH Supplemental Publishers Inc.

GO ON

Champion of Civil Rights

7   Dr. Garcia set out to combat these injustices. He believed that all Americans should have the same rights.

8   In 1948, Dr. Garcia formed a group called the American GI Forum. He especially wanted to help those who served in the war. In 1949, a war hero named Felix Longoria died. His wife wanted to hold a service for him at a funeral home, but the director refused because the Longorias were Mexican-American. With the help of Dr. Garcia, the American GI Forum, and Senator Lyndon B. Johnson, Felix Longoria was buried with full honors in Arlington National Cemetery.

The Highest Honor in the Country

9   Throughout the 1950s and 60s, Dr. Garcia and the American GI Forum worked tirelessly for equal rights for Mexican-Americans. Due to their hard work, discrimination decreased. Mexican-Americans were welcomed in public places and earned positions in government.

10   In 1967, Dr. Garcia was appointed as an ambassador to the United Nations. A year later, he became the leader of the U.S. Commission on Civil Rights. In 1984, Dr. Garcia earned the highest award in the nation, the Presidential Medal of Freedom.

11   Even while Dr. Garcia fought for civil rights, he still worked as a doctor in Corpus Christi. "El Doctor," as he was called, never turned away a patient who could not pay. He worked well into his 70s, healing the sick and fighting for civil rights.

© HMH Supplemental Publishers Inc.

GO ON

22 The Garcia family moved to Texas —

F to help Mexican-Americans
G to avoid being teachers
H to visit family in Texas
J to escape the war in Mexico

23 Dr. Garcia fought for civil rights because —

A he was a war hero and wanted to continue fighting
B he needed to do something besides being a doctor
C he was not allowed in movie theaters
D he saw how poorly Mexican-Americans were treated

24 How did the author organize this selection?

F By expressing an opinion about civil rights
G By describing the events in Dr. Garcia's life
H By comparing Dr. Garcia and Felix Longoria
J By explaining how to organize a civil rights group

25 In paragraph 6, the word <u>rampant</u> means —

A limited
B out of sight
C widespread
D unpleasant

© HMH Supplemental Publishers Inc.

GO ON

26 What is the importance of paragraph 9 to the selection?

F It shows that the issue of civil rights is no longer important.

G It explains how Dr. Garcia became a doctor.

H It shows that Dr. Garcia had come a long way from a small Texas town.

J It shows that hard work can accomplish big goals.

27 Which sentence from this selection **BEST** explains why Dr. Garcia called his group the American GI Forum?

A *Mexican-Americans still struggled.*

B *In 1948, Dr. Garcia formed a group called the American GI Forum.*

C *He especially wanted to help those who served in the war.*

D *Due to their hard work, discrimination decreased.*

28 Look at the chart of information from the story.

| Dr. Garcia enlists in the U.S. Army. | Dr. Garcia helps the Longoria family. | _____ | Dr. Garcia works as a doctor into his 70s. |

Which event should go on the empty box?

F Dr. Garcia forms the American GI Forum.

G Dr. Garcia's parents leave Mexico.

H Dr. Garcia earns the Medal of Freedom.

J Dr. Garcia goes to The University of Texas at Galveston.

© HMH Supplemental Publishers Inc.

GO ON

29 The reader can conclude that the Longoria case —

A received national attention
B was important to Dr. Garcia, but not Senator Johnson
C cost the funeral director his job
D helped Mrs. Longoria, but no one else

30 The author wrote this selection to —

F inform the reader about an important leader
G encourage the reader to become active in politics
H entertain the reader with a story
J persuade readers to become doctors

31 One idea from this selection is that —

A success depends on luck
B you should stand up for what you believe in
C family is most important
D health is more important than wealth

32 Which of the following is the **BEST** summary of the selection?

F Hector Garcia grew up in Texas. His parents encouraged him to get a good education. He went to medical school and became a doctor.
G Hector Garcia's family came to Texas from Mexico. Hector believed in equal rights for everyone. He grew up to become a doctor and an important civil rights leader.
H Hector Garcia was a war hero. He enlisted in the U.S. Army during World War II and earned the rank of Major. He won many medals.
J Dr. Garcia formed the American GI Forum. Felix Longoria's wife could not have a service at a funeral home. Dr. Garcia helped Mrs. Longoria. Felix was buried in Arlington National Cemetery.

© HMH Supplemental Publishers Inc.

GO ON

**Read this selection. Then answer the questions that follow it.
Fill in the circle of the correct answer on your answer document.**

Letter to the Editor

April 22, 2010   Section B

1   Today is Earth Day. Instead of seeing *green*, I am seeing *white*. So much *white* that I'm seeing RED! White, you see, is the color of most plastic bags. After years of the "Reduce, Reuse, Recycle" campaign, why are plastic bags still everywhere?

2   Plastic bags come from petroleum, a type of fossil fuel. Fossil fuels are "non-renewable resources" because they take millions of years to form. Every year, Americans throw away about 100 billion plastic bags. That's like dumping twelve million barrels of precious oil. Plus, when plastic bags are made, greenhouse gases pollute the air.

3   Plastic bags contribute to our growing litter problem. They are eyesores on our streets. They clog storm drains and sewers, and wash into rivers or oceans. There are about 46,000 pieces of plastic floating in every square mile of ocean. There is an area twice the size of Texas between California and Hawaii called the Eastern Pacific Garbage Patch. Millions of pounds of trash swirl in its <u>currents</u>, and most of it is plastic.

4   Plastic bags can harm animals. Turtles and other animals sometimes mistake floating plastic bags for tasty jellyfish. The animals choke when they try to eat them, and many die. Animals can also get trapped in plastic bags. More than a million birds and 100,000 marine animals die every year from plastic.

5   Why should we care? Remember that fish and seafood are important food sources for many people. Let's say a jellyfish eats some plastic and then a fish eats the jellyfish. Then a fisherman catches the fish and it ends up on your dinner table. Plastic bags are made of petroleum. They contain toxins such as lead and mercury. Petroleum, lead, and mercury don't sound very appetizing to me!

6   Because plastic bags are durable, they're hard to get rid of. When a plastic bag ends up in a landfill, it's there for a very long time. Scientists estimate that a plastic bag can take 20 to 1,000 years to decay! Even though plastic bags can be recycled, only about two percent of plastic bags are recycled in the U.S. Nearly all plastic bags end up as trash.

7   What should we do? Some cities and countries have banned plastic bags. In Bangladesh, in 1998, floodwaters drowned most of the country. Water could not drain because plastic bags clogged the drainage systems. In 2002, the country banned plastic bags entirely. In the U.S., San Francisco was the first city to ban them and others have followed.

Continued on next page

GO ON

© HMH Supplemental Publishers Inc.

8

Letter to the Editor *continued*

Other cities and countries charge a fee for plastic bags instead. In Ireland, people pay 33¢ per bag. Due to this fee, there has been a 90% decrease in the use of plastic bags since 2002. Shoppers in Seattle are now charged this same fee for plastic or paper bags.

9

It's time for our city to ban the bags! Plastic bags are convenient, but we don't need them. We need a clean city and environment. Call on City Council to pass a law banning plastic bags. Bring reusable cloth bags to stores. Recycle the plastic bags you have now. These steps will help make every day Earth Day!

33 Look at the following diagram of information from the letter.

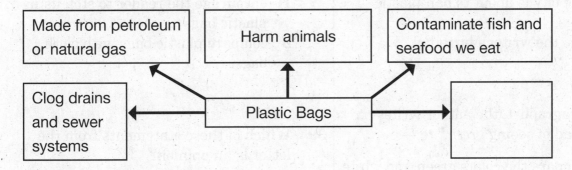

Which idea belongs in the empty box?

A Are hard to use
B Better than paper bags
C Are inconvenient
D Take a long time to decay

© HMH Supplemental Publishers Inc.

GO ON

34 In paragraph 1, the author writes "I'm seeing RED!" to show that —

F the author likes the color red
G the author is blushing
H the author prefers the color white
J the author is angry

35 What is the importance of the particular date on which the author wrote this letter?

A It is Earth Day.
B It is when the newspaper allows letters from readers.
C The city is about to ban plastic bags.
D It is the writer's birthday.

36 In paragraph 1, the author writes "Instead of seeing *green*," to —

F compare the colors green and white
G associate green with Earth Day
H contrast Earth Day and the color red
J suggest using green and white

37 Paragraphs 2 through 5 are mainly about —

A how much plastic bags cost
B how convenient plastic bags are
C how plastic bags harm the environment
D how strong plastic bags are

38 The author wrote this letter to —

F inform the reader about non-renewable resources
G entertain the reader with stories about sea animals
H encourage the reader to stop using plastic bags
J compare plastic bags with cloth bags

39 Which of these statements from the letter is an opinion?

A *There are about 46,000 pieces of plastic floating in every square mile of ocean.*
B *In Bangladesh, in 1998, floodwaters drowned most of the country.*
C *Today is Earth Day.*
D *It's time for our city to ban the bags!*

© HMH Supplemental Publishers Inc.

GO ON

40 Look at the dictionary entry below for the word <u>current</u>.

> **current**\kər-ənt\ *noun* **1.** a body of fluid moving in a direction **2.** a flow of charges of electricity **3.** the general course, trend *adj.* **4.** up-to-date

Which definition represents the meaning of <u>currents</u> in paragraph 3?

F Definition 1
G Definition 2
H Definition 3
J Definition 4

41 How can this letter best be described?

A It is completely factual.
B It offers opinions supported by facts.
C It only includes the author's opinions.
D It is mostly fictional.

42 The author probably wrote "These steps will make every day Earth Day" to —

F encourage readers to protect the environment all the time
G suggest that we have a daily holiday
H promote the use of plastic bags
J encourage people to wear green

© HMH Supplemental Publishers Inc.

STOP

Practice Test 2

> **Read the writing prompt. Use your own paper to follow the steps for responding to a prompt.**

> Write an essay about a person you admire.

The information in the box below will help you remember what to think about when you write your composition.

> REMEMBER—YOU SHOULD
> ❑ write about a person you admire
> ❑ write a main idea sentence that tells who the person is
> ❑ write detail sentences that tell what this person did and why you are writing about this person
> ❑ try to use correct spelling, capitalization, punctuation, grammar, and sentences

© HMH Supplemental Publishers Inc.

GO ON ➡

> **Read the introduction and the passage that follows. Then read each question and fill in the correct answer on your answer document.**

Terri wrote a report about opossums. She would like some help revising and editing her report. As you read, think about the changes you would make. Then answer the questions that follow.

The Opossum

(1) Many people think opossums is related to rats because of their long tails, but this is not true. (2) Opossums are marsupials. (3) A marsupial is a type of mammal that carries its young in a pouch. (4) When the babies have matured enough. (5) They left the pouch. (6) They will then rode on the mother's back until they are old enough to be on their own.

(7) These nocturnal creatures sleep during the day are active at night. (8) Opossums are omnivores, which means that they eat both plants and other animals. (9) They eat a great variety of insects, and they eat snails, and they eat grasses, and they eat leaves, and even fruit. (10) On ocashion, they will eat snakes and rodents. (11) Some rodents are nocturnal.

(12) Some people are afraid of opossums, but they shouldn't be. (13) They are gentle animals that prefer to be left alone. (14) Because they eat garden pests and rodents they are very beneficial. (15) If you happen to see an opossum strolling at night, leave it alone. (16) Be glad it is there to eat any unwanted pests.

---

1 Which sentence does **NOT** belong in the report?

A Sentence 3
B Sentence 8
C Sentence 11
D Sentence 14

2 What change, if any, should be made in sentence 1?

F Change *tails* to **tales**
G Change *their* to **there**
H Change *is* to **are**
J Make no change

GO ON

© HMH Supplemental Publishers Inc.

3 What is the **BEST** way to rewrite sentences 4 and 5?

A When the babies leave, the pouch has matured enough.

B When the babies have matured enough, they leave the pouch.

C Leaving the pouch. The babies have matured enough.

D The babies, leaving the pouch. Have matured enough.

4 What change should be made in sentence 6?

F Change *their* to **her**

G Insert a comma after *back*

H Change *rode* to **ride**

J Change *rode* to **riding**

5 What revision, if any, is needed in sentence 7?

A These nocturnal creatures, they sleep during the day and are active at night.

B These nocturnal creatures sleep during the day. And are active at night.

C These nocturnal creatures sleep during the day and are active at night.

D No revision is needed.

6 What is the **BEST** way to revise sentence 9?

F They eat a great variety of insects, snails, grasses, leaves, and even fruit.

G They eat a great variety of insects. They eat snails. They eat grasses. They eat leaves. Even fruit.

H They eat a great variety of insects, they eat snails, grasses, leaves, and even fruit.

J Make no change

7 What change, if any, should be made in sentence 10?

A Change *they* to **them**

B Delete the comma after *ocashion*

C Change *ocashion* to **occasion**

D Make no change

8 What change, if any, should be made in sentence 12?

F Change *afraid* to **afriad**

G Change *shouldn't* to **should'nt**

H Delete the comma after *opossums*

J Make no change

9 What change, if any, should be made in sentence 14?

A Change *Because* to **However**

B Change *beneficial* to **binificial**

C Insert a comma after *rodents*

D Make no change

GO ON

© HMH Supplemental Publishers Inc.

> **Read the introduction and the passage that follows. Then read each question and fill in the correct answer on your answer document.**

Shira wrote this story about her vacation. She would like you to revise and edit it. As you read, think about the changes you would make. Then answer the questions that follow.

A Vacation Out of This World

(1) I worked very hard in science and math this year. (2) When my Dad saw my report card, he grinned from ear to ear and said "Shira, you've earned a very special vacation. (3) I think you would enjoy a trip to the Johnson Space Center in Houston, Texas when school is out in June. (4) What do you think?"

(5) I have always dreamed of flying in outer space so I shouted with joy, "Absolutely, Dad! (6) The Space Center, that will be awesome!"

(7) The movies were so real that we could actually feel what it is like to blast off into space! (8) There was hardly much to see, do, and learn at the Space Center. (9) In the Mission Status Center, we could see astronauts in space and listen in on their conversations.

(10) The most fun of all was the Living in Space module where visitors could really see what life is like for astronauts living aboard the space station. (11) Because astronauts float around a lot, it's difficult for them to eat. (12) And difficult to sleep. (13) And take a shower. (14) We learn these fun things and more!

(15) My visit to the Space Center showed me what it really takes to become an astronaut—a lot of hard work. (16) I'm inspired now. (17) I'll continue to work hard on science and math, and maybe my dream of becoming an astronaut will come true.

© HMH Supplemental Publishers Inc.

GO ON ➡

10 What change, if any, should be made in sentence 2?

    F Delete the comma after *card*
    G Insert a comma after *said*
    H Delete the comma after *Shira*
    J Make no change

11 What change, if any, should be made in sentence 3?

    A Insert a comma after *trip*
    B Change *June* to **june**
    C Insert a comma after *Texas*
    D Make no change

12 What is the **BEST** way to revise sentence 6?

    F The Space Center now that will be awesome!
    G The Space Center will be awesome!
    H Awesome, the Space Center will be!
    J Make no change

13 Which sentence could **BEST** be added before sentence 7?

    A We took a tram to see the old rockets.
    B When we first got to the Space Center, we watched movies about shuttle missions.
    C Alan Shepard's flight in 1961 lasted only 15 minutes.
    D I wish that I could go to the Space Camp in the summer for kids.

14 What change, if any, should be made in sentence 8?

    F Change *at* to **of**
    G Change *hardly* to **so**
    H Delete a comma after *see*
    J Make no change

© HMH Supplemental Publishers Inc.

GO ON

15 What change, if any, should be made in sentence 9?

   A Delete the comma after *Center*
   B Change *astronauts* to **Astronauts**
   C Change *conversations* to **conversashuns**
   D Make no change

16 What is the **BEST** way to rewrite sentences 11 through 13?

   F Because astronauts float around a lot, it's difficult for them to eat, sleep, and take a shower.
   G Because astronauts float around. All the time, it's difficult for them to eat, sleep, and take a shower.
   H Because astronauts float around a lot. It's difficult for them to eat, sleep, and take a shower.
   J It's difficult. Because astronauts float around a lot, to eat, sleep, and take a shower.

17 What change, if any, should be made in sentence 14?

   A Insert a comma after *both*
   B Change *learn* to **learned**
   C Change the exclamation point to a question mark
   D Make no change

18 What change, if any, should be made in sentence 15?

   F Change *showed* to **show**
   G Change *what* to **which**
   H Change *really* to **realy**
   J Make no change

19 What revision, if any, is needed in sentence 17?

   A I'll continue to work hard on science. And math and maybe my dream of becoming an astronaut will come true.
   B I'll continue to work hard on science and math and maybe. My dream of becoming an astronaut will come true.
   C I'll continue to work hard. On science and math. And maybe my dream of becoming an astronaut will come true.
   D No revision is needed.

© HMH Supplemental Publishers Inc.

GO ON

© HMH Supplemental Publishers Inc.

> **Read the introduction and the passage that follows. Then read each question and fill in the correct answer on your answer document.**

Maya went to a festival and wrote this report about it. She wants you to help her revise and edit the report. As you read, think about the changes you would make. Then answer the questions that follow.

Festival of the Moon

(1) In many Asian cultures, a great festival is held in autumn when the moon were at its biggest and brightest. (2) This full moon occurs near the autumnal equinox, a time when night and day are almost equal in length. (3) This full moon is also called the Harvest Moon. (4) During the bright Harvest Moon. (5) Farmers can work even at night.

(6) The festival is a joyous one during which families got together to view the moon. (7) According to one legend, the Old Man in the Moon knows everyone's future. (8) Young and old alike clime on hilltops and gather in parks or other open spaces to look at the moon. (9) They hope that the Old Man will grant their wishes. (10) There is also a Woman of the Moon named Chang'e. (11) She is a favorite subject of legends and poems.

(12) Children love this festival. (13) They are allowed to stay up past midnight, parade with colorful lanterns, and eat special foods. (14) I have never been to a parade before. (15) Sweet, round cakes called moon cakes eaten and tea is sipped by people while admiring the moon.

---

20 What change, if any, should be made in sentence 1?

    F Change *great* to **grate**
    G Insert a comma after *moon*
    H Change *were* to **is**
    J Make no change

21 What change, if any, should be made in sentence 2?

    A Add a comma after *occurs*
    B Delete the comma after *equinox*
    C Add a comma after *day*
    D Make no change

GO ON ➡

22 What is the **BEST** way to combine sentences 4 and 5?

  F During the bright Harvest Moon, farmers can work. Even at night.

  G During the bright Harvest Moon, farmers can work even at night.

  H During the bright Harvest Moon farmers working even at night.

  J During the bright Harvest Moon, farmers will work. Even at night.

23 What change, if any, should be made in sentence 6?

  A Change *got* to **get**

  B Change *joyous* to **full of joy**

  C Insert a comma after *together*

  D Make no change

24 What change, if any, should be made in sentence 7?

  F Change *everyone's* to **everyones'**

  G Change *knows* to **know's**

  H Change the period to a question mark

  J Make no change

25 What change, if any, should be made in sentence 8?

  A Change *clime* to **climb**

  B Change *alike* to **a like**

  C Insert a comma after *hilltops*

  D Make no change

26 Which sentence could **BEST** be added after sentence 11?

  F In one legend, Chang'e was so light that she floated to the moon.

  G The festival began about 3,000 years ago in China.

  H The Jade Rabbit is often found on moon cakes.

  J China launched a space craft named Chang'e in 2007.

27 What is the **BEST** way to revise sentence 15?

  A Sweet, round cakes are eaten because tea is sipped while admiring the moon.

  B People eat sweet, round cakes. Tea is sipped by people. While admiring the moon.

  C People eat sweet, round cakes and sip tea while they admire the moon.

  D Sweet, round cakes eat and sip tea while admiring the moon.

28 Which sentence does **NOT** belong in this story?

  F Sentence 5

  G Sentence 10

  H Sentence 12

  J Sentence 14

© HMH Supplemental Publishers Inc.